The Unexpected Gift

WHAT MY MOTHER'S DEATH TAUGHT ME ABOUT LIFE

By

CAROLINE DINNALL

Published by hope*books
2217 Matthews Township Pkwy
Suite D302
Matthews, NC 28105
www.hopebooks.com

hope*books is a division of hope*media

Printed in the United States of America

First paperback edition.
Paperback ISBN: 979-8-89185-092-7
Hardcover ISBN: 979-8-89185-093-4
Ebook ISBN: 979-8-89185-094-1
Library of Congress Number: 2024941908

hope∗books
hopebooks.com
Because the world needs your hope-filled words now more than ever

Endorsements

"In how many ways can the Body of Christ speak about and walk through the grief of losing a loved one? Had it not been for John the Apostle who, with just two words, modeled the breadth of grief when he wrote "Jesus wept" (John 11:35), we would be left to think this mountainous emotion capable of excavation and exegesis. If you have lived it, you know that this is not the case. If you have yet to live it, you will and at that point, you will see what I mean. Grief is inescapable and must be lived out fully. Caroline understands this. In this book, she travels her experience, leaving no bend unturned or door closed; she enters every room and sits there and waits for us to come in and sit with her. Like Jesus weeping, she too, knows the power of presence and welcomes all who feel grief's pangs to not feel it alone."

CHRISTINA LEVY

"God hears and responds! This book confirms this fact as well as assures us that His promises of never leaving us is real. Even in death God is with us on the journey and is still hearing our pleas as we transition. What an amazing glimpse of what it is like to move from this life to the next. The account of Caroline's mother heals a grieving heart."

MELODY BROWN

"This book is a profound exploration of grief and loss, capturing complex emotions and the journey to find God amid pain. Through deeply personal reflections and spiritual insights, Caroline offers wisdom and comfort, making this book a must-read for anyone seeking hope and healing in the face of profound loss."

CHERYL NEMBHARD
Author, Speaker, TV/Podcast Host
and Executive Director of Women Speakers Collective

To my mommy, Nysley May Bryan Dinnall. Thank you for being the inspiration for this book, and thank you for giving me the gift of your legacy.

To the rest of my immediate and extended family, we are truly a blessed people. I love you.

To anyone dealing with the loss of a loved one, I know it's hard to accept that they are gone forever, but they've left so much behind. May you discover the unexpected gift that births from your grief.

Table of Contents

Memories
The details of life,
That never seems to fade away.
What we cling to,
To secure an inner satisfaction,
And lasting contentment,
That we once thought were lost.
Memories.

Memories: A Preface

We won't remember every single precious moment we've ever lived. So what does that say about those we do remember? I say there's something awfully important to take away from those memories. Something to learn that may impact the quality of our lives forever.

There are memories that we simply picture in our minds—let's call these "scotch tape" memories—and that stick with us for long periods. We remember some details and those involved, but after several years, dust invades the sticky side of the scotch tape—that's our memories—and we forget the distinct details that made this memory so special in the first place.

Then there are the "super glue" memories. The memories that—well, you guessed it—stick like glue. These are the memories we can feel, smell, hear, and see all at once. It's as if every last detail happened just yesterday.

There are also good memories and bad memories: the birth of a child and witnessing their first steps, losing your first tooth, riding a bike, experiencing your first day of school, going to Disneyland, flying on a plane, getting married, losing a loved one, attending their funeral. The list goes on.

I have a question for you. What about those bittersweet memories that lay in between the good and bad? You know, those memories that first suck the joy out of you yet somehow leave a tiny sprinkle of hope and newfound strength inside of you.

Can I tell you one of mine?

It was a sunny September morning in 2010. My father, brother, and sister had already left the house to start their days. I was still at home, sleeping calmly and still. Then, my alarm clock went off. I'm not talking about the alarm clock on your cell phone or the classic alarm clock that sits on your side table, no. This was a human alarm clock.

This was my mother. She'd been my human alarm clock for as long as I can remember, whether I had to get up early for school on a weekday or church on a Sunday morning. She would storm into my room without knocking, jump into my bed, and swarm me with tickles and kisses. Then she would cuddle beside me, and we'd talk about life. When we both felt it necessary to get up and conquer the day, we would. That made us late a few times. Maybe more than a few times. Or maybe more than that.

I wish I could tell you that was how I got out of bed that September morning, but it wasn't. Yes, my mother was still my alarm clock, but the disturbing sounds of nonstop dry coughing prompted me to jump out of bed that morning.

My mother had been battling stage three lung cancer.

She had always been my superhero. I've always admired her undeniable strength, wisdom, and passion to inspire others. She was my beauty, wisdom, resilience, and creativity standard.

I'll never forget the feeling of my heart skipping several beats moments before stepping into my mother's room that morning. I found her sitting up in her bed, gasping for air. I rushed towards her and propped her pillows, doing anything I could to make her feel comfortable in this moment of discomfort.

All she needed me to do was get her a glass of water. And so I did.

When I returned with that tall glass of water, my mother began to tell me about a supernatural journey she had experienced moments before physically waking up that morning. Burning with excitement, she told me that this experience would change her life forever.

I begged my mother to hold the details of this mysterious journey until I could find the new hand recorder I had stored in my room for my high school journalism class. I unpacked it from its impossible-to-open plastic case and ran back to my mother's room, recorder in hand. I joined her cross-legged on her bed. With the utmost anticipation, I held out my recorder. Little did I know, I was holding the key that would later unlock an unanticipated version of me.

I was ready to soak in every detail of the experience my mother longed to share with me.

Pause. Rewind.

At this very moment, you're probably wondering, *what gave Caroline the urge to stop her mother from sharing her journey just so that she could find a hand recorder?*

Some might say I was obeying the voice of God. Others might say it was the heart of a true journalist that lived inside of me—or that I was just super excited to use my new hand recorder for the first time. Looking back on that day, I truly believe that my decision to do such a thing was a *God* thing. And I'm stickin' to this belief.

Who would have thought that an 18-minute recording would change my life forever?

SHE'S GONE

Fast forward.

A month after that September morning, Mom was gone forever: October 29, 2010. What happened on this day came as an unexpected and unpleasant surprise to all who knew the sweet soul I got to call Mommy.

I had our whole lives planned out.

She would take hundreds of photos with me at my high school graduation.

She would be the proud mother at all three of her children's weddings.

She was going to help raise her beautiful grandchildren.

I had it all timed out perfectly.

I have humbly come to accept that my timing and God's timing are completely different.

Time alone does not heal. Even after several years, I still miss my mother every second of every day. Sure, I might cry a little less. But every once in a while, the sad memory of her last day on earth plagues my mind, and I can't help but take a few moments to soak in my grief.

Wishing I could just see her again. Cuddle with her in my bed again. Hear her voice again.

I would pull out that recorder when I felt down and defeated or missed my mother. Each time I listened, I experienced a beautiful exchange with God. Every word spoken reminded me that there was still so much to live for, even after loss.

The September morning communion encapsulated in the form of an 18-minute recording—now a "super glue" memory shared with my sweet mother—has caused me to see life from an entirely new perspective.

The next several pages contain my mother's words that morning, transcribed. From here on out, we will call this journey Mom's "first-class trip," as she liked to call it.

What She Said to Me

1

Before you read this, I want to let you know that these were my mother's exact words that September morning. I removed some aggressively repetitive parts but still kept most of them because I want you to feel like she's talking to you, too. Enjoy this sweet journey.

"The First-Class Journey"
Transcribed from Audio by Nysely Dinnall (UNCUT)

Listen to the full audio recording at:

thelifejournal.ca/book-exclusive

"Yeah, so, the worship songs, all of the songs I can't remember, but all I know is I was worshipping. I was praising God. I don't know; even before I was being pulled out of bed, I just sensed a presence, and I just started praising God. I just sensed something. I just sensed that God was there. I sensed a sweet, sweet, sweet, sweet presence, and I started praising God. And then the particular sound that I remembered after I woke up was, 'Sweet Jesus'—I remember how I said it in the dream. I said it with such passion. It's like He was right there, and I was talking to Him. I said, "Sweet Jesus, Sweet Jesus, what a wonder You are/You are brighter than the morning star/You are precious as gold..." Then, all of a sudden, the song just started fading, and I started moving off of the bed. There's nobody there, but it's like somebody was pulling me, but I couldn't see anybody pulling me. And I was straight, just straight, going, you know? It was like somebody was pulling—pulling! I saw even the sheets pulling, and nobody was there. And as soon as I came off of the bed—there's nobody holding me up—I'm air bound. I'm just going, going! I hit the hallway, and I said, "Oh dear Father—oh, bye, family," and I remember turning my head. It's like I'm through the hallway. I said, "Oh, bye, family," and then as soon as I said that, it's like I'm in a tunnel, like all by myself, and I'm just going, going, going faster than the...oh my God, faster than a jet, like lightning. Just going so fast. So fast. And I was still straight. I wasn't walking, or I wasn't going up, I was just going straight—straight (laughs), and then it's like, I guess my family was still on my mind because I said, "But Lord, I need some more time with my family—I need some more time with my family! Give me more time; I need to say bye!" And as soon as I said that, as soon as that came out of my mouth, my spirit was back in my body. I didn't feel anything. I just woke up as soon as I said that. But look how quick! After I was going so fast, whatever it was, in a split second, you know? And look how fast I was travelling—lightning going through, and as soon as I said that, the Lord returned me. He knew my heart, and you know, what I'm glad about is that I wasn't selfish. I didn't ask to come back for anything of my own. I asked Him to come back so I could spend more time with my family. And so I felt so happy because I could have asked Him for anything else, but I asked Him to give me more time with my family. And He did! I truly believe I am healed. He healed me for that purpose: to spend more time with you guys (chuckles). He's a great God. He's a great God! But it's an awesome journey. Nice. It's nice (laughs). There's no fear, Caroline. There is no fear. You don't need to fear (coughs). No fear. It was such a sweet journey. It's like, my goodness, it's nothing that I've ever experienced. And you know, even though I was going, I wasn't troubled. In my heart, I was sort of happy because I knew that I was going to see the Lord. My expectation was to see the Lord—like—that made me happy. There's no fear. It was such a good journey. It was such a wonderful journey, you know? So I guess there is nothing to fear after this life. There is nothing to fear. It's just happiness. There is nothing to fear. But I'm thinking, oh my gosh, why didn't I just go to heaven, see heaven, and then come back (laughs hysterically)? I should have gone! Maybe He would still bring me back (giggling) because, you know, after I said, "I should just wait and go see heaven and then tell Him I want to go back and see my family," I probably wouldn't want to come back! But you know the thing is, what if I didn't say, "I want to come back to see my family—" I wouldn't, you know? What if I didn't say I wanted to come back? 'Cause it's the moment I said that that I came back, you know! Otherwise, I'd still be on my journey! So, oh my goodness, wow, you see, ask, and it shall be given, eh? Ask, and it shall be given. Even at the end, when you're headed for heaven, you can still ask, and you'll be given what you ask for. Ask, and it shall be given. Wow. It's not a thing to fear; it's something to embrace and welcome. Honest to goodness. Oh my God. It's so nice. So nice. It's like you're travelling first-class all by yourself (big laugh). YES! It's like you're travelling first class all by yourself, and oh my gosh! Oh, dear Lord, I don't know. It was amazing. It was an amazing experience. I don't know what popped into my head, why I said, "Lord, my family! I need to spend more time with my family." Why, you know? There had to be something important about the family that He returned me, you understand? There has to be. What is it? You know? It was hilarious because as soon as I said that, the journey stopped, and I woke up immediately. When you have a dream, sometimes you wake up and you don't remember. It was so vivid that I remember everything. God is good. Maybe He's just showing me the future. He's just showing me what would happen, or He's giving me a taste of what will happen. I guess He's trying to let me know that there's nothing to fear. It's something to welcome, to invite. I leave myself in the hands of God. I know God is a healer; I have no doubts. Like the three Hebrew boys said, "If our God will not deliver us, we will not bow." It's the same thing. I know God is a healer, but if He chooses not to, then it's something I have to accept, and maybe He's trying to show me that it's not such a bad thing (laughs). I guess He sees my heart. That's the only thing that I'd really want is to spend time with my family. He saw my heart. He saw my heart—that my family was my concern. He saw my heart, and He answered me according to my request. I have no doubt that I'm healed, and I'm going to spend a lot more time with my grandchildren—maybe even my great-grandchildren, and He's saying, "If you don't, it's not that bad—it's not that bad at all." It's a very nice journey. I felt so nice going through that journey, so I can imagine what it was like at the end of that. I can only imagine. The ride itself was so amazing HA-HA! Oh, my Lord! Caroline, the presence that I felt around me was like nothing I've ever experienced. And it's not like I'm seeing anybody, but the feeling of what I get, the vibe, it's awesome! I just wanted to go and see Jesus. That's what I felt like. Oh my goodness, I felt like my heart was just anticipating seeing Jesus while I was going through that tunnel. It's amazing! It's AMAZING! Oh, my Lord! There is nothing at all to fear after this life! It's just niceness after this, just pure niceness. Niceness, niceness, niceness, I'm telling you. Nothing, nothing at all to fear. Nothing man. (Caroline: "People need to hear this"). I know. (Caroline: "I want to experience this.") No, you don't need to experience that because you are not in the position I am in! Your time will come, Caroline. You will serve Him right, and your time will come. He knows what He's doing. Everybody has their own timing, everybody has their own blessing that they will receive, and sometimes God just needs to just, you know, put you through some stuff so you know that He's there. Sometimes we believe that He's not there, you know, but He is! And sometimes, He just brings these things upon you to show that indeed He is there, and indeed, you are going to a better place. He knows how to encourage, and this is one of the ways He did it to encourage me. He's so real. He's so real, Caroline. He is so real. He is so real. And you don't have to see Him. You just know. When you're in the spirit, it's like you're connected to Him. It's like there is a connection that can't be explained. It cannot be explained by the flesh. Because when I was going through that tunnel, I knew He was there. I didn't see Him. I knew His presence was around me. And I knew, even before it was happening, I started praising God because there was a presence there, and my spirit felt it. My spirit felt it. My spirit knew that it was His presence. It's not like I was strange to it. My spirit knew the presence right away, and as soon as I felt the presence, I just started praising God. Even though I didn't see Jesus I was saying, "Sweet Jesus," and I was smiling. It's like I was talking to Him because He was right there. And the way I said the words, it's like I'm talking to Him directly. And then I remember saying, "Oh dear God—," 'cause it's like I knew I was going to heaven. I said, "Oh Lord, wash me, Oh Lord, cleanse me, purge me, preserve me!" I was just asking the Lord to clean me up before I got there! It's amazing! And then, on my way there through the tunnel, just lightspeed, I said, "But Lord, I need to spend some more time with my family (laughs). Give me more time, Lord!" All of a sudden, I woke up. In a split second, from traveling so fast, I woke up. A split second. Amazing."

How Grief Crept Up on Me

2

What comes to mind when you think about the word *grief?*

I only fully understood the impact of grief when it found me personally.

To me, grief has always had a look. When I think of grief, I see the most miserable, gloomy-looking day. Heavy clouds, dark skies from morning to night, and not a peek of sun in sight. A massive downpour of rain and scattered showers in between.

It's just plain sad.

Before losing my mother, it was a word I had mostly heard at funerals or a concept discussed in a Biblical context. For example:

"Surely he has borne our griefs and carried our sorrows..." (Isaiah 53:4, ESV).

Or this popular scripture:

"For his anger endureth but a moment; in his favour is life: weeping may endure for a night, but joy cometh in the morning" (Psalm 30:5, KJV).

Grief was described as unpleasant, heavy, and even unbearable. But even though it was described as such, it was something

> WHEN I LOST MY MOTHER, GRIEF WAS NO LONGER JUST A WORD OR A LOOK. IT BECAME A VERY REAL EXPERIENCE OF A DEEP, SUDDEN, AND UNEXPECTED HURT.

that Jesus would relieve us from. So, although hearing the word "grief" in this context on countless occasions made me aware of this very human experience, it left me assuming that it was something that was never fully my responsibility and something that would quickly pass over.

What a rude awakening I experienced when grief crept up on me.

When I lost my mother, grief was no longer just a word or a look. It became a very real experience of a deep, sudden, and unexpected hurt.

Grief is the feeling of having your breath taken away again and again, all while still very much alive. It's creating wells of water with your seemingly unending teardrops on any given day, in any given place, at any given time. It's constantly spacing out mid-conversation without a care or clue. It's constantly replaying scenarios in your head about how this very feeling of grief could have been avoided and how you could have played a huge role in its reverse.

Grief felt like punishment.

THE YEAR OF FIRSTS

I don't believe anything can truly prepare anyone for the Year of Firsts after a loss. The Year of Firsts is the year you are constantly reminded that everything is not as it once was. It's the year of uncomfortable adjustment, where the sudden holes in life that come with loss don't give you a break.

The first day is spent thinking about the rest of your life without the one you've lost.

The first sleep.

The first text message you start to type and then suddenly remember won't ever be received.

The first recital without them.

The first birthday without them.

The first—insert a big milestone—without them.

The hardest for me was the first Mother's Day—and it's likely still the hardest day to face to date. You may be thinking, *how does Mother's Day trump your mother's birthday or the day she died?* It's the day that reminds me of how well my mother mothered myself and my siblings.

It's a day set aside to reflect on the benefits of a mother's love and care—when even just speaking of her brings about a palpable feeling of comfort.

I don't remember every detail of my first Mother's Day without my mother, but I do remember the endless tears that fell down my face.

I remember how hard it was to be on social media (mostly Facebook at the time) as friends and family would post their favourite photos and share their fondest memories and thoughts about their mothers or mother figures. I was gutted and envious. I kept internally asking the million-dollar question: "No, but seriously, why me? Why *my* mother?"

I felt left out—a sense of FOMO, if you will. As much as I wanted to share about my awesome mother, I felt it didn't hold as much weight as those whose mothers were still alive. That was definitely a first.

I'd always felt a sense of pride when sharing my family with the world, whether it was through sharing stories about them in conversations with others or posting a picture with an endearing caption on social media. Around this time, celebrating my mother in these ways felt unsettling, as if I was vying for attention and pity. In hindsight, and after much reflection, I realize I wasn't. In actuality, it was all a part of my grief process—(I just didn't know that yet).

Sharing about my mother during my first Mother's Day post-loss was a way for me to reflect on the beautiful memories, life lessons, and principles my mother left us before transitioning. It was also an opportunity to show the world that one can live on after loss, and, that though I was still coping, I had not fully lost all hope.

This was an important one.

I quickly developed an interest in helping others who would also experience loss (basically everyone at some point), and I wanted to find a way to ensure that, if it were possible, they would never have to go through the degree of pain that I did alone.

Although Mother's Day was one of the more difficult occasions to celebrate without my mother, it wasn't the only one.

The first household birthday celebration with my family was another. Singing *Happy Birthday* would never be the same.

On the first Valentine's Day, my mom didn't come home with chocolates to remind me that I was loved just as much as everyone else. Finding something to truly be grateful for with an aching heart was hard on the first Thanksgiving. On the first Christmas? That goes without explanation.

My mother's absence, specifically in the first year, brought about a grayness and a dullness to the most exciting life events. Sadness heavily clouded over the joy stored up within me that was meant to shine. Anxiety that grew from the discomfort of our new normal stole the peace that we were promised. The sparkle of a "special" day would become the dust spec of just another day.

Looking back, it felt as though the raw emotion and pain that came from these firsts would latch on to me for a lifetime—much like many of the clothes in my closet. I know I'm not the only one who struggles with seasonal closet purging—or at least I hope I'm not the only one.

I understand the necessity of a good purge once or twice a year, but I have to admit that it isn't the easiest task for me. What makes it so challenging?

First, clothing items have become a few sizes too small over the years. I hold them in the crevices of my closet with high hopes of one day sliding back into them after losing weight at some point in my lifetime. Next are the items that need massive alterations—the items I've convinced myself I could fix on my own—if only I made the time. Then, there are the eclectic pieces that I felt were oh-so-cool in the store but oh-so-not-cool at home and oh-so-don't work with anything else in my wardrobe. Finally, there are the items of clothing that hold sentimental value. With just one look, try-on, or smell, they bring me back to the memory that initially made it oh-so-special.

I've always been a bit of a fashion gal. But personally, clothing and fashion haven't always been about how I look—although that remains an important factor.

For as long as I can remember, I've always been intrigued by textiles and the many techniques used to weave thread together to make garments. It's no secret I jumped at my first opportunity to learn all about the history of fashion in grade 10 and aced the class—but that's another story for another day.

I have always been intrigued by the stories that clothing can tell. I would be the one to stay up late with a magazine and flashlight under my sheets to read about a designer's backstory on how a long-lived family tradition inspired their new Fall line. Storytelling through clothing is one of the reasons why I think I'm an expert people watcher. There's something thrilling about how one's fashion choices influence one's life journey. Maybe that's why clearing my mother's closet was so hard to do after losing her.

CLEARING MOM'S CLOSET

The thought of clearing my late mother's closet made me sick to my stomach. It's one of those things that doesn't even cross your mind until someone says to you:

"It's time."

In this case, my aunt and Godmother graciously assisted in helping my family carry this heavy load—pun intended. My first thought was, *already? How could I?*

Clearing my mother's closet felt disloyal and dismissive. It had only been a couple of months, and the thought of my mother being gone for good hadn't even registered yet.

Why did we have to clear out this space so quickly? Why couldn't we let it linger for a little while longer?

My siblings and I searched Mom's closet and selected the items we wanted to keep. I, for one, felt so incredibly guilty, like I was abandoning my mother. I felt forced to move on by locating everything that reminded me of her and choosing to remove them from my life, give or take a few things.

When you lose someone you love, it feels like you've lost it all.

The natural response to such a loss is to hold onto everything left and never let it go. We almost become ruthless in holding our grip on anything that is near and familiar because it allows us to feel as though we have managed to savour the remains of what we deem as normal, or 'life as it was before the sudden change.'

I guess that's why throwing my mother's belongings away, even if it was a simple handkerchief, made me so uncomfortable.

A TIME TO REFLECT

Take a moment to think of the person or people you've loved and lost. Then, answer these questions for yourself. Jot some notes down as you go.

1. What items have you kept in remembrance of your loved one?

   _____

   _____

   _____

   _____

2. When you observe them (touch, smell, sight), how do they make you feel?

   _____

   _____

   _____

   _____

3. Do these items evoke any particular memories? What are they?

   _____

   _____

   _____

   _____

Like the seasonal purging of my own closet, I struggled with purging my mother's closet for slightly different reasons.

One: Some items in my mother's closet reminded me of sticky memories I had shared with her in the past. For example, there is a beautiful white, frilly halter top that she used to wear. It looked lovely on her, and every time I saw her sport it, I could tell she had a little extra pep in her step. It made her feel confident and powerful—clothes can do that sometimes. One day, I glimpsed her as she charged to the front door on her way to work.

I asked, "Hey Ma, you look gorgeous! Where are you headed?"

"To work," she replied.

"In those fancy clothes?" I asked.

"Of course, Cara. You don't have to wait for the special days to wear special things. Life is short—wear them now!"

That's a life lesson I still cling on to. Now, whenever I "over-dress" for a casual night out and someone asks me why I did so, I can just chuckle and respond by saying, "Why not?"

Thanks, Mom.

Two: There were items in my mother's closet that reminded me that I'm truly *her* daughter—and that made me so proud, yet also reignited a type of sadness that we couldn't fully live out our shared uniqueness. While purging, I found a baby pink and black dress. Sounds normal, right? Wrong! The top of the dress had a polka dot pattern, and the bottom had stripes. Imagine the contrast of the colours and patterns all mixed together. What do you get? Chaos, beautiful chaos.

Keeping this item from my mother's seemingly endless closet was a no-brainer because it reminded me that we share something special: distinctive taste in fashion. It was our "thing," and I didn't notice it until then.

That's one thing I can say grief is good for. It allows you to face unusual scenarios that open your eyes to the little details that shape who you are as a result of your connection to a single human being.

Three: Items in my mother's closet represented the milestones we celebrated with her. The last huge milestone our family celebrated together was her 50th birthday.

I remember the moment she walked in with my brother to the song *Isn't She Lovely* by the great Stevie Wonder. She was quite the sight in her a-line, rhinestone-bodice, floor-length dress—and had the most brilliant smile to match. To see her soak in all the love from that night was like unexpectedly finding a mom 'n pop ice cream shop on a hot Sunday evening.

Sweet.

So I had to keep that dress. It only felt right. I even wore it once, and I felt the love.

Four: There were items in my mother's closet that reminded me of her signature scent, according to me. Random as ever, I kept a pair of her white and pink tropical fleece pyjamas because they smelt like a body oil she used to apply most nights before going to bed. On nights when I would lay beside her before going to bed, this is the scent I smelled. Smelling this scent while clearing out Mom's closet was comforting. I never wanted to forget beautiful moments like those when laying beside my mother was a reality, not a memory. The distinct scent of this oil was the closest thing to this past reality.

Clearing my mother's closet took a full day. A long, frustrating, reminiscent, joyful, hard, full day. But it also felt like it went all too quickly.

It was hard for my soul to keep up with the pace of the day. We went through mountains of clothes and shoes, and in minutes—sometimes in seconds, had to decide whether to place an item in the "keep," "donate," or "save for later" pile. If I had it my way, I would have decided to walk through this chapter of life after loss a little slower. I probably would have waited six months to a year to face Mom's closet, or I would have broken this task up into more than one day. Perhaps a week or so.

While clearing my mother's closet is now a distant memory, I still hold a few lessons from this time close to my heart. These lessons have silently influenced how I maneuver life today. Let's walk through them together.

CLEARING MY MOTHER'S CLOSET REMINDED ME OF THE FRAGILITY OF LIFE.

I saw things that I had just seen her wear less than a month prior. One moment, she was there wearing these items, and the next moment, she wasn't, leaving them behind. Our ignorance of human mortality can lead us to believe that death, to whatever degree, won't hit us next.

We assume it will always be the workmate, acquaintance, or anyone else before it's us. Holding my mother's clothing in-hand was the rude awakening that indeed confirmed such a thing could—did—happen to me, too. On the other side of loss, I'm more empowered to appreciate present moments as often as I can remember.

Goodbyes are more intentional.

Celebrations mean everything.

Moments spent are treated tenderly.

Everything changes when life is seen and understood as fragile.

Clearing my mother's closet reminded me that the things that don't have life in them still have a way of bringing life to seemingly dead situations.

Certain items surfaced beautiful life experiences that brought waves of deep emotion—all from a shirt, shoes, or a pair of pyjamas. It's amazing how simple items like these, once branded by their owners, leave such a lasting mark on those left behind. They have a way of restoring memories. They help us grieve.

Clearing my mother's closet reminded me of the power of having a village and community of support. We go much further when we're together than when we're apart. Tackling my mother's closet was never a thought until my aunt and Godmother brought it to my attention. I didn't think I'd be able to make it past five minutes rummaging through my mother's belongings, but five minutes quickly turned into several minutes and then into hours. This was all possible with the company and encouragement of loved ones.

The journey of grief isn't meant to be a lonely one. One who hasn't hiked before shouldn't climb Table Mountain in Cape Town, South Africa, for four and a half hours alone. It's uphill, steep, rocky, and extremely intimidating—trust me, I've done it (but thankfully, not alone). If you can do it with company, I can confirm that in the end, it's rewarding, but only after hours of encouragement, crying, pushing, drinking lots of water, and perhaps having some serious life-changing conversations on your way up.

On the other hand, if you try to hike this mountain alone, you'll likely talk yourself out of it very quickly and miss out on the satisfying feeling of making it up to one of the most beautiful sights in the world—in my opinion.

While walking through grief, we need people who will show up, speak life into us when we are down, and reach out and help us when we fall (Ecclesiastes 4:10).

It is in the safety of our handpicked village that we receive the gentle thrusts forward we need to push past levels of pain that grief often deals us. It is in the safety of our village that we experience the hand, beauty, and love of God in the most challenging times.

Looking back, I genuinely believe that God had His hand on the timing of clearing my mother's closet.

I believe He knew how hard such a thing would be for all of us and loved us enough to uncover the fresh wound, clear it with peroxide, and finish off with a bandaid in record time. He knew we wouldn't be able to bear this pain unattended for too long. Some aspects of the grief process require us to *just do it*, like Nike, because if we don't do it now, we never will (effectively anyway).

Sometimes, you just have to *do it* during the grief process. Otherwise, you will find yourself drowning in the weighty sorrow of a degree of your past you've been overdue to conquer. Sometimes you have to move on from things even when it feels premature so that you can avoid crippling yourself, to face *your* next. There will be bigger giants to face in your next, but it will be even more difficult to overcome with the heavy weight of your past.

With that being said, I must acknowledge and reiterate that as diverse beings, it is inevitable that we will all grieve differently. This may have been a chapter in my family's process that had to move quickly, but that might not be the path and story for you. Some things still take time, and that's okay. Perhaps there is another grief chapter in your story that will require a swifter pace.

How do you know where you sit on the spectrum of "I'm ready" and "not yet?" I believe a good place to start is by asking yourself the following questions:

1. Have you truthfully accepted the loss of your loved one, as hard as it may be?
2. Is your reluctance to close a chapter in your grief journey stunting your ability to progress in life? For example, when cleaning a loved one's closet (assuming you lived with

them), do you find it depressing or distracting to walk into the closet or even pass by it? Does this immediately affect your mood for the day? *Of course, this is a very reasonable reaction at the outset of your loss, but it is worth assessing if it continues for an extended amount of time.*

THE FIVE STAGES OF GRIEF AND BEYOND

Elisabeth Kübler-Ross developed the five stages of grief in her bestselling book *On Death and Dying*. She speaks from the perspective of patients who walk through the five stages of dying from a terminal illness. Before passing away, she was passionate to warn the public that these five stages were only meant for the dying. While I respect and understand the intent, I wish I could sit down with her and tell her how familiar the grief stages of the dying felt to me. I can see how easy it is for society to misconstrue the intent of these grief stages to fit the narrative of people who lose loved ones. How? Because losing someone you love can feel like death itself—to some degree. I've observed Kübler-Ross' brilliant framework, and the nerd in me couldn't resist sprinkling in my interpretation of the five stages of grief from the perspective of a griever, living with loss. Let's dig in.

Denial

I'd like to define this grief stage as the Shock stage. At this point, it's inconceivable even to think that the person we've lost is actually gone forever. *No, this is not true; this could never happen to me. This* is an example of our internal dialogue. This refusal to believe is a defense mechanism that can only last for so long until reality forces its way in. Kübler-Ross quotes a subject in her book who says, "We can not look at the sun all the time. We cannot face death all the time." Kübler-Ross breaks this quote apart from the perspective of patients at the onset of learning about their terminal illnesses: "These patients can consider the possibility of their own death for a while, but then have to put this consideration away in order to pursue life."[1]

A patient can linger in the thought process of *this couldn't be* for as long as they want to; after all, they are human. However, at some point, looking at the issue at hand (the sun) for too long will eventually burn their eyes, and dwelling on the possibility of death for too long will literally sap the life that's left within them.

The same goes for us who've experienced loss. Yes, we have the right to wrestle with the loss head-on, to ponder on the how, ask all the questions, and even deny that what's happening before us is real, but after a while, we must lean into the truth—that we've lost, and that nothing can change that now. All we *can* do is choose to go on with the uncomfortable reality of this fresh loss and commit to pursuing the life that waits for us on the other side.

In the Denial stage, it's normal to feel unhinged. I felt like a madwoman. What did this look like, you ask? It looked like calling my mother's phone, just to see if there could be any possibility that she'd answer—even though we had her phone at home with us. It also looked like walking in crowded spaces and mistaking the figure of a stranger for her physical body. In this stage, our minds don't allow us to accept our reality until we say, "Green light, it's actually happening." If we don't say this ("green light"), we could eventually start to form false and alternate realities.

I guess that's another reason why we shouldn't stare at the sun too long.

Anger

I call this grief stage the "Cat Out of the Bag" stage. It's when we've long exhausted our denial and can't hold on any longer.

---

1 Kübler-Ross, Elisabeth. *On Death and Dying.* Scribner, 1969, 35.

Then, what replaces that denial is "anger, rage, envy, and resentment." In simpler terms, everything that's been happening inside (that denial has been safeguarding) bursts out simultaneously. The anger of grief comes from the sudden and unwanted confrontation of an unfortunate interruption in our lives. We are angry because something happened to us (or to the one we love) that we never asked for or imagined would happen at a time when we weren't prepared for it. This anger is like a dark cloud that sits over our lives. Everything happening around us is an immediate annoyance or threat to our joy.

In this stage, I felt myself becoming numb, not only to my own circumstances but to others'. For context, I would feel threatened if and when I saw people, whether I knew them or not, enjoying a moment with their own mothers. I'd think to myself, *I can't believe they're doing this in front of me—have they no decency? Well, I guess they better enjoy that while it lasts; before they know it, their mother will be snatched away from them, and they'll end up just like me.* Of course, I kept this inner dialogue to myself, but what deep pain I was in to be so terrible, even in thought, to those who have done me no harm?

I was also furious at God. The inner dialogue went a little like this: *How could you do this to me, Lord? I believed You. I prayed. I left it all in Your hands. What did I do wrong? Are you punishing me?* Since I didn't get what I thought I should have (my way), it was not too long before it became harder to trust God, pray, and believe in His "good" will for my life. How could the Lord's will for my life be good when He took away something, someone, that was so good to and *for me?* The Anger stage is one that, in a way, highlights one's selfish nature. Me me me. My my my. My struggle. My sadness. My hurt. My life, My mom. It's no wonder Paul urges us to "rid ourselves of all such things as these: *anger*, rage, malice, slander, and filthy language from our lips" (Colossians 3:8).

Bargaining

Kübler-Ross explains this stage mainly from the perspective of the dying. In this stage, the dying make bargains with God. They say things like, "I'll be a better person, I promise, just please get me out of this, God!" For this book and its quest to support the individual grieving a loss, I'll explore the typical Bargaining stage of the griever.

Let's call this the "Back-and-Forth" stage. You know the tee-ter-totter that you used to spend ample time on at the park? Envision this, except it's all happening in your brain, and you're bargaining with yourself to land on the most logical reason for your loss. You keep going back and forth, trying to come up with multiple combinations of how your loved one's journey to death unfolded. You think of ways this could have been avoided or instances that may have further contributed to the unfortunate outcome. The Bargaining stage is a terrifying and exhausting stage to endure.

In my Bargaining stage, there were a couple of staple formulas that constantly ran through my head:

If I had done X more, Y would have happened, and Z would have been the final result.

Or:

X caused Y, and I must face Z for the rest of my life (Z being my mother's permanent absence).

This stage consists of a lot of blaming. Blaming myself. Blaming others. It also includes a lot of "if-only"s.

If only we had admitted Mom to a better hospital.

If only we had better doctors to care for her.

If only I were at the hospital before she died to pray a prayer of healing that would change everything.

If only.

If only.

If only.

I wish I could say this stage quickly passes over or has a defi-nite end before the next stage. Unfortunately, I can't. The truth is, it will likely chase you for longer than you expect and as long as you let it. But to save your brain from the constant runaround, I think it's important for you to know that all your reasoning won't necessarily get you the answer. It will only temporarily soothe your longing desire to know the answer.

Depression

We'll call this stage the "Stage of Intense Emotions." Ac-cording to Kübler-Ross, the wave of depression that occurs in this stage is a result of the dying being "unable to do something about or salvage" their terminal illness. She breaks down the two types of depression: reactive depression ("feelings of regret, sor-row, leaving behind the world and the people you love, not being able to fulfill dreams, etc.") and preparatory depression ("taking into account impending losses before the dying dies, or the pos-sibility of death").[2] For us grievers, this stage can similarly bring about feelings of regret, sorrow, loneliness, and hopelessness. It feels as though there is no turning back or recovery from the re-ality of our loss. It's officially settled in, and we feel alone, as if we are drowning in a sea of open water in the middle of the night with no night lights. We can't feel the bottom or where anything begins or ends.

We try to refrain from drowning, but we can't swim. We ex-pend so much energy, trying everything we can to stay afloat for as long as possible. We enter into an intense stage of ongoing fa-tigue. There is nothing left to give at some point amidst all of the thinking, reasoning, and bargaining. We lose all the physical and

---

2 Kübler-Ross, On Death and Dying, chap. 6.

mental strength required to make the loss of our loved ones make sense. And when hope loses its grip, some of us feel at peace with drowning.

After some time, I began to tell myself that the world was okay with losing my mother because everyone else was moving on as normal. I then started to believe that maybe the world would be okay with losing *me*. I felt that the best version of myself was Caroline with a present mother. I knew of no other life, and I wanted no other life.

While thoughts of leaving this world on my own account flooded my mind, I never chose to act. Thankfully, I couldn't fully bring myself to such a place. While this may be seen as a type of victory to an outsider looking into my life at this stage, internally, it felt like torture. For 24 hours, over and over again, I had to live in a world where I felt my presence was no longer necessary.

The Depression stage is very real. Before even moving to the next section, if you are experiencing any emotions similar to those explained in this stage, I encourage you to put this book down and consider seeking help from a friend, family member, helpline, or licensed therapist. You can also send me a message if you have no one to whom you can turn. I'm always open to talking and helping point you in the right direction.

You don't have to go through this alone.

Acceptance

This is "The Indifferent But OK" stage. At this point, we are "neither depressed nor angry;" we lay somewhere in between. As Kübler-Ross puts it, a terminally ill patient would have already passed through feelings of "envy, anger, mourning, and fatigue,"[3] but the same goes for us grievers. In this stage, we can't run or hide anymore and are backed into the corner of truth. It's

---

3 Kübler-Ross, On Death and Dying, chap. 2.

happening. But the fact that we can accept the truth of our reality doesn't necessarily mean that we are happy about it. We accept but still don't know how to feel and choose to embark on the journey of the unknown, hoping it leads to some sort of clarity.

Most would assume that this stage allows us grievers to take a final sigh of relief. While this can be true, an internal battle still remains. It's not easy to accept that our loved ones have passed on, and accepting this truth almost feels like betrayal.

This stage was a blur for me. To this day, I'm unable to pinpoint the exact moment I fully accepted that my mother had passed on. Was it at the funeral? Or a few months later? Or five years ago? This may be hard to believe, but the reality is that sometimes the Acceptance stage pays you a visit more than once. I often found myself *thinking* I had accepted my mother's death for good when, in reality, my acceptance was temporary. It's one thing to accept, and it's another to accept and believe.

Over time, I accepted and believed that my mother had passed on from this earthly world for good. I finally understood that it was my responsibility to find a way to live without her there. I still needed to learn what that could or should look like. At the time, I had no definite blueprint or step-by-step manual to walk me through this new life, and I had yet to learn if there was even one. All I could do was accept my present reality and figure it out from there, one day, one step at a time. That's all that's required of us grievers: the tenacious ability to accept what is before us and commit to saying yes to living the rest of our lives.

***

Most people would stop here and be satisfied. They'd think, *OK, cool, I've gone through all the five stages myself; I guess that means I'm a normal human being with normal feelings and experiences.* But I'm not like most people, and if you haven't yet noticed, I like to think a lot. Maybe too much sometimes. So, although I can confirm that these five stages of grief are, in fact, true and very much reflective of the human grief experience, there are a couple of stages missing, in my opinion. I'm no doctor of the human sciences, but I am a human of lived experiences. Hear me out on what I would call the two bonus stages of grief.

Guilt

Much like the Bargaining stage, the Guilt stage is where we grievers tend to linger over a long period, mulling various scenarios and possibilities. We try to reason and problem-solve in our minds, but in this bonus stage, our thoughts and ponderings are taken a step further—into the deep end.

Guilt is the thief of peace. At this point, it is difficult for us to navigate a central and lasting peace while going through the motions. Peace is replaced by anxiousness, shame, self-punishment, and fear.

Let's break each of these peace thieves down practically through my personal grief experience:

Anxiety. After my mother's passing, I would often think about the times I could have spent with her while she was still alive, times we could have spent doing ordinary things. I was still attending high school, hanging out with my friends, and serving in various capacities that regularly took me outside my home.

My mother did a great job of ensuring we didn't worry about her too much, even on her worst days. Sometimes, I would catch her being untruthful about her sickly state in a moment and try to step in and help the best way I knew how. Other times, I would take her at her word and go about my days as normally as I could.

Don't for a moment think I didn't feel the moths of guilt in my stomach. I sure did, but I also wanted to respect my mother's wishes to shoo me away so that I could live my best teenage life amidst her battle with cancer. Sometimes, it felt like living "normally" was the best thing I could do—for myself and my mother.

And sure, that worked while she was still here, but imagine the anxious thoughts that rushed over me when I realized my time with her had suddenly run out.

They rushed through like a gushing spring. Thoughts like:

How wicked of me to go to school while my mother was dying!

How stupid of me to walk away from Mom based on her position— even if she said to go.

Those thoughts tormented me, but I eventually realized that my mother's desire for me to live my life was her way of protecting me and allowing me to have a semblance of normalcy.

Shame. I wasn't present for my mother's final breath, and that was a tough pill to swallow. In fact, for a long time, it felt like the pill was oversized, and I had no water to even wash it down. The shame didn't just come from not being present. It also came from the fact that I had been on my way to an event that evening, even though I knew she was in the hospital at the time. I felt uneasy about going out, but my mother and family reassured me everything would be alright. The plan was to go straight to the hospital afterward, or even better, Mom would be back home by then.

That was the expectation.

The reality was that I didn't make it, and I carried the burden of absence and lateness with me for what felt like an eternity.

Self-punishment. There's a twisted mental logic that we, unfortunately, subject ourselves to when it comes to losing the ones we love or even seeing them in pain. It's that "me instead" mentality—you've seen it in the movies, particularly action movies. The damsel is in distress, kidnapped by the bad guys, and her prince, her king, and her knight storms into the room where she is held at gunpoint and says, "Take me instead!"

That's how we grievers cope in the Guilt stage.

We would rather feel the pain or even die than face the pain of seeing the ones we love die. Guilt grows within us and says, *it should have been me.*

That's what I said.

This emotional response is renownedly known as "Survivor's Guilt." Here's an example: someone is in a car accident with two others, and they are the only one who survives. They keep having flashbacks, and it's tough to move past what happened. It may be hard for them to understand why they weren't affected. This is a sad reality that haunts many of us grievers.

Fear. Believe it or not, there is a category within guilt felt after experiencing the loss of a loved one that can heighten one's fear of man. It's common for those who witness our grief processes to pick it apart and make assumptions about our feelings as we walk through one of the most difficult seasons of our lives.

Outside conclusions and projections can overwhelm us, making us feel as though our natural response to grief is flawed or incorrect. This can lead to severe isolation or the desire to hide our true emotions from the public (like walking around with a poker face that can't be easily read)—both very destructive practices.

I remember, on a couple of occasions, being told that I didn't cry enough after my mother's passing. I remember being asked why I didn't do *this* or *that* while I was grieving. I began to think I wasn't honouring my mother in her absence. I quickly learned that the opinions of others I carried were just that—opinions and careless projections. Though it took some time, I've been able to dispose of this fear as it relates to how I grieve. Now I know that I can freely grieve the way I know how.

My friend, grief is subjective. There is no one way to do it—or go through it. Reject the temptation of the fear of man. Guard against the careless projections that try to slither into your ear and take root in your heart. Allow yourself to grieve the best way you know how, and never, ever apologize for it or dumb it down for the comfortability or acceptance of others. Don't allow fear to cripple you or interfere with your journey to recovery.

The Guilt stage would fit perfectly between Stage 3: Bargaining and Stage 4: Depression. This is because it carries on from bargaining and can lead to depression if not tightly harnessed.

Dream

The Dream stage is exactly what it sounds like—a dream. Though it is not always the first topic of discussion, having multiple dreams of a loved one after loss is a very common occurrence for the typical griever. I have had many conversations with fellows who have experienced significant loss, and the types of dreams that they have about their loved ones offer unique modifications yet somehow string together with the types of dreams I've had. Examples of these modifications include seeing a loved one years younger or years older than they were when they passed on, in no pain, in a specific location that has meaning to either them or those they've left behind. I think there's something to gather from that: Our dreams play a role in how we see our loved ones after they've gone on.

Over a span of 13 years, I've had a few dreams of my mother. They were beautiful, yet frustrating. Beautiful because I was able to see her face clearly again, just for a few seconds. Frustrating because in those few moments of dreaming, I felt like the world was back to how it should have always been or how I desired it to be. I thought, miraculously, that my mother was back in my life for good. But it was all just a dream.

There was one dream in particular that I will never ever forget. There was no dialogue. Just my mother, walking solo in a silk blue dress. She turned to me, her head just above her shoulder and her eyes looking straight at me. She smiled—and I woke up. Ugh!

What I found interesting about this dream, in particular, is that my mother looked much younger in the dream than when I had last seen her. She looked as if she was in her early 30s. She was bright-eyed and joyful. She looked so content and peaceful. I woke up wondering why I had dreamt of her at that age, why the bright blue dress, and why she was so happy. I never got the answer to this.

When the ones we've loved and lost frequently cross our minds, there is a greater chance we may dream of them. And as a believer, I don't believe dreams are just dreams. I believe that everything God creates and allows has a meaning and purpose. He created mankind, and we've been given the ability to dream, just like those who have gone before us. Joseph had dreams (Genesis 37). Solomon had dreams (1 Kings 3). David had dreams (1 Chronicles 28). Each of their dreams were a foretelling of a significant occurrence. A famine. A mandate to lead an entire nation. A quest to build the temple of God in Jerusalem.

What am I getting at here? Perhaps my dream of my mother was God's way of foretelling her whereabouts. Perhaps He was trying to tell me that she would end up right where she needed to be—with Him. What if the silk blue dress represented a type of fresh start, freedom, or calmness with the Father? What if her smile symbolized her joy and peace with where she was headed after her earthly life; no pain, no suffering?

What if.

I don't have all the answers, but one thing's for sure, my God is intentional, and so are the dreams He allows us to carry, especially for us grievers.

I would plant the Dream stage right after Stage 5: Acceptance.

THE NEXT PART

Throughout my grief journey, I've received countless revelations about practical life morals that I believe every person should live by to supplement and sustain a fulfilling life.

In the following chapters, I want to share these revelations with you. A compilation of my reflections over the years, all deriving from one distinct memory: the 18-minute miracle recording of my mother's first-class journey.

Consider each chapter a detailed journal entry that recounts and reflects upon my mother's unique journey with Jesus, accompanied by my personal interpretation of what her experiences have taught me about life—as I know it now.

I pray that you read this next part with an open mind and an open heart.

Ready? Let's fly.

The Treasured Bonds of Family

'm a bit of a hoarder. I was a light hoarder before I even knew what hoarding meant.

My hoarding days started in my youth. On outdoor field trips and family ventures to the park, a day wouldn't go by without finding and collecting rocks. But not just any rocks. These rocks were uniquely shaped. Some resembled the human face. Some were heart-shaped. Some were glittery. I felt like a gold miner. Something about rocks intrigued me: the rigid edges that grazed my fingers, how they glimmered under the sunlight, and how the gray, white, peach, and brown tones of the rocks effortlessly complimented one another. We frequently visited the beaches when we travelled for vacation during the summer months—often to Jamaica or Florida. For a mineral hoarder like me, this was a jackpot gold mine. I left with my pockets full of shells and a plastic water bottle, ziplock bag, or compartment of my bag full of sand. It would be nice to say that I was storing these items to gift to some friends back home in Canada, but this wasn't the case. I was storing it all away for myself.

I've even saved my baby teeth.

There's a touching backstory to this:

Around eight years old, I felt a sudden and sharp pain in my mouth. A day after the discovery, the sharp pain turned into excruciating pain that my little mouth couldn't handle. My dentist scheduled an immediate procedure with a specialist to remove this troublesome tooth.

They warned me that my tooth would be quickly extracted from my mouth and separated from its family of pearly whites. Imagine the horror that plagued my mind leading up to the big event.

"I'm going to put this mask on you in a few moments, and it will spray out gas that will put you to sleep. We are doing this so that you are completely knocked out during the procedure and unable to feel anything."

"Nothing at all?" I asked for safety.

"Nothing," he confirmed.

I remember everything fading to black. *Then,* I remember feeling a heavy-duty lever forcefully yanking my tooth out of my mouth. *Twist, twist, pull...*

SCREAM!

The specialist left me with celebratory candies for making it through my very first surgery ever. Along with that, I received a bag of supplies to help me heal and the little bugger that got me into this mess, my baby tooth—root and all.

I took a good look at my extracted baby tooth for the first time and thought, *how could this little itty bitty thing cause so much pain?* I also thought, *how fascinating.* I was successful in saving my last few baby teeth. I think I still have them somewhere in my storage.

I kept most of these keepsakes—the rocks, sand, sea shells, and teeth in a purple shoebox for years, and over time, my hoarding legacy expanded a great deal.

My taste in hoarding levelled up with age. Now, I hoard journals, memorabilia from family and friends, and celebratory cards.

Looking back at these keepsakes evokes efficacious emotion. To reminisce on my reflective, sometimes cringey thoughts on paper from past years, take a few moments to marvel at an international souvenir a friend bought me, or read the heartfelt words written in a birthday greeting card from years past. I keep these things to preserve the beautiful memories they brought about and to relive somehow the priceless moments that left me feeling warm inside upon first interaction.

I know I'm not the first person to do such a thing. Maybe you have a hoarding habit of your own, collecting cool socks, mugs, books, or card collections that you hold near and dear to your heart. How does holding onto these things make you feel?

Take a few seconds to ponder.

You'd be happy to know that people practiced the concept of collecting and storing items for memories' sake thousands of years ago (1400 and 1370 B.C., to be exact). I spoke to a friend about my deep thoughts on memories, and they began to shed light on the fact that God cherishes memories, too.

There's a story in the bible about God splitting the Jordan River (a 251-kilometer-long river in the Middle East) for people in Israel so that they could continue their journey to what was called The Promised Land. Joshua 4:1-7 (NLT) says:

> "When all the people had crossed the Jordan, the Lord said to Joshua, "Now choose twelve men, one from each tribe. Tell them, 'Take twelve stones from the very place where the priests are standing in the middle of the Jordan. Carry them out and pile them up at the place where you will camp tonight.'
>
> So Joshua called together the twelve men he had chosen—one from each of the tribes of Israel. He told them, "Go into the middle of the Jordan, in front of the Ark of the Lord your God. Each of you must

pick up one stone and carry it out on your shoulder—twelve stones in all, one for each of the twelve tribes of Israel. We will use these stones to build a memorial. In the future your children will ask you, 'What do these stones mean?' Then you can tell them, 'They remind us that the Jordan River stopped flowing when the Ark of the LORD's Covenant went across.' These stones will stand as a memorial among the people of Israel forever."

God orders His people to build a monument to commemorate a significant event and remind generations of His goodness and faithfulness to His people. I find this fascinating, not only because I closely resonate with the deed of collecting rocks in my childhood but also because I can't help but believe the theme of family and legacy is effortlessly woven into this story as well. Twelve stones for twelve tribes, all stacked together to form a massive souvenir of remembrance for future generations to behold and find meaning and purpose in. It is a sacred souvenir for a moment in history.

Part of me hopes that my hoarding collections will mean something to my future bloodline and kin. Maybe they will one day hold my collection of shells from beaches and lakes worldwide or read the pages of my century-old journals and feel a sense of pride, gratefulness, or responsibility to continue a rich legacy. I confidently say "rich" because I am proud of the legacy passed down to me by my family—and no matter what the nature of your passed-down legacy might look like, you should find something to be proud of, too.

It was after my mother's death that all of these hoarded things became so much more valuable to me. They were no longer things I liked and wanted to keep. They became the memorabilia that shaped who I was. They became the memorabilia that held me together when my world fell apart. Occasionally, I would hold these items in my hands and reflect on the times that made them so special.

When we lose those we love, there are seasons where almost everything we do and say is filtered through our loss.

While looking down at these hoarded items, I couldn't help but think about the countless smiles, laughs, and frowns they once brought to my mother's face each time I shared them with her for the first time. I guess holding onto these distinct memories felt just as tangible as holding onto the hoarded items themselves.

I believe that's why we grievers like to hoard—we hold onto the things we do, especially after losing those we love. Something about them resurfaces the part of us that was content with how life *was*—if even for a moment.

It's hard to let go after a loss. We feel we've already let go of enough.

BIRDS OF A FEATHER FLOCK TOGETHER

One summer evening at a local lake in Ontario, Canada, I saw a massive flock of seagulls flying in the clear blue sky—the most I've ever seen together. I fixed my eyes on them, amazed by their ability to fly in one accord.

It wasn't by chance that they could fly together so effortlessly; it was by nature. Each seagull knew their place and how to stay within their bounds. They understood that they were but one small detail of a bigger picture. They understood that they were stronger with their flock than they could ever be alone. But even on their own, they knew how to be effective and useful and carry themselves in the same confidence they had when in the large flock.

How did they know to do this? I suggest that once a seagull knows their place in the flock, they know their place in the world. Could it also be true that once people know their place at home, they find their place in the world?

I think it's about time you get to know a little bit more about my tribe. There was a sitcom about an African-American family based in Brooklyn Heights that often played on our TV. There was a particular episode when the mother and her several children do a musical performance of *The Night Time is the Right Time* by Ray Charles[4] in their living room in celebration of her and her husband's 49th wedding anniversary. Bright smiles and excitement filled the room. I remember the joy I felt while watching this scene for the first time. It felt so familiar, as if it was my family on the screen, even though their world was fiction and my world didn't exactly replicate theirs.

I could match each of my family members to a character on the screen as I watched, which brought so much joy to my soul. You could imagine the thrill I'd later experience when family friends would see our small tribe leaving or entering our place of worship on Sunday mornings and stop us in our tracks to tell us how much we'd reminded them of the Huxtable family on *The Cosby Show.*[5]

I could surely see what they saw. The joy, the togetherness, the way we came alive when we'd sing and dance to our favourite tunes. Almost every family birthday celebration ended with a new rendition of *Happy Birthday* and a freestyle dance in our kitchen.

I'd like to think that music played a part in my parents' meeting. On September 30, 1960, my mother, Nysley May Bryan, was

---

4   Charles, Ray. *"(Night Time Is) The Right Time." The Genius Sings the Blues,* Atlantic Records, 1961.

5   *The Cosby Show.* Created by Bill Cosby, performances by Bill Cosby, Phylicia Rashad, and Malcolm-Jamal Warner, NBC, 1984–1992.

born in St. Catherine Parish, Jamaica. Two months after birth, as custom for many families in Jamaica, Nysley was picked up from her mother's house every Sunday by her Aunt Yvonne, who brought her over to visit her extended family.

One Sunday, while dropping off baby Nysley back at home, Aunt Yvonne asked Nysley's mother if she could keep Nysley. Along with her parents, Doris and John Bryan, she wanted to care for her. Without hesitation, Nysley's mother packed her child's bags and sent her off to live with Aunt Yvonne for good.

I know what you're thinking.

How could a parent so easily ship their child off without a care? Apparently, a decision like this isn't difficult to make when you lack the resources to care for your family. Maybe my grandmother realized this was the best thing she could do for my mother. Perhaps she saw a pocket of opportunity for my mother that she could not provide.

Church was a way of life in Jamaica. Whether or not parents went to church, their children never missed a week. Mom and her cousins attended Sunday school at West Prospect New Testament Church of God. In her adolescent years, she got baptized and quickly found a way to get involved in ministry.

With the help of family, Mom eventually moved to Canada. She worked as a nanny and, of course, continued her quest in ministry at a local church. Mom was a youth leader with a sincere heart to pay it forward and help guide young people on their life journeys.

But she was mostly known as the songbird at church; she led worship and directed the choir. Serving the Lord meant everything to her. My Aunt Melody once shared her admiration for my mother's faith and dedication to serving God and His people: "She was extremely generous with her time and resources. She's been my example in so many ways throughout my own Christian journey. She taught me about the importance of tithing. Even when she had 50 cents daily for lunch, she faithfully gave her tithe."

As a young adult who spent most of her time at church, it only made sense that she met my father, Lester Dinnall, there. Lester played bass guitar, and Nysley led the congregation in hymns and songs—an obvious match made in heaven, right?

Just picture it. Nysley, in her bold and beautiful Sunday best. Her eyes, bright, and her voice, one of an angel. She looks over her right shoulder to direct the band backing her up and suddenly locks eyes with a tall, dark, and handsome man with killer jerry curls, a three-piece cream suit, and a shiny top-of-the-line bass guitar in hand.

Back in Jamaica, it was custom to fashion nicknames for friends and family members. Mom's nicknames were "Cleopatra" and "Sissy Perch," both attributing to her large eyes that pierced encountering souls. I can't help but think something about her big brown eyes captured my dad's attention.

The real story is that Dad had been admiring Mom for quite some time before they met. He told me it was her driven, can-do attitude that drew him to her the most. He greeted her with a shy "Hi, Sister Bryan" every chance he could get. They became more familiar with one another over short and sweet conversations at the bus station on their way home.

Several phone calls, dates, and good times led to intentional courtship. And what do they say about the rest? History.

Eight months later, the music-loving lovebirds tied the knot and wasted no time to start a family with music-loving babies.

I'm pretty sure my siblings and I emerged from the womb singing sweet melodies. For as long as I can remember, the three of us sang on the big stage at church to serenade the congregation with a gospel hit and encourage the people on Sunday mornings.

My brother Brian sang tenor, my sister Alicia sang alto, and little 'ole me carried the soprano.

I remember the nights we would prepare for Sunday morning ministry. Dad would find his guitar to guide us, and Mom would coach us on how to sing the song right and confidently. Our rehearsal sessions would turn into a mashup of random, freestyle family fun. We always knew how to have a good time.

Brian and Alicia were 13 days shy of being Irish twins. They were best friends. They did everything together—crazy things, scary things, fun things, all things. According to my parents, my debut in the family brought some peace to the chaos. I was the calmest baby out of the three of us.

I was also a rainbow baby. Mom had a stillborn birth a year before I surprised her. His name was Andrew. I always wondered what life would be like with him. If we'd grown up close-knit like Brian and Alicia did—or if, as a result of his successful entry into the world, I would even be here today. I often wonder how painful it might have been for Mom, physically and mentally, to excitedly push out the purpose that had been brewing within her for months, only to say goodbye moments later.

I'd liken this feeling to my experience of losing my mother. How painful it was to hold out on hope and build up my faith, believing that God would heal Mom once and for all, only to lose her months later.

Tragic.

Yet, even in the tragedy, life can find its way back in very unexpected ways. For my mother, the loss of a child later became the unexpected gift of me. And for me, the loss of a mother became the unexpected gift of a renewed perspective on life and its true meaning. Losing my mother led me through a tunnel of deep desire to learn more about the *flock* I've been divinely placed in. I felt myself desiring to reflect on my family history more than ever. That desire to dig deep has led to further discovery of myself and those I love.

And in discovering more about those I love while grieving the loss of my mother, I realized that the ability to grieve is actually a privilege. To feel the impacts of loss so deeply means that I've loved, and I've loved hard.

I've loved hard enough to feel emotions so strongly when I lost.

The loss meant something.

The loss changed me.

The loss left a mark on me.

To grieve means that those we've lost truly meant something to us. To grieve means that there are countless memories we've been able to store away over the course of knowing those we've lost, memories we can reminisce on for the rest of our days.

To grieve means that the love was real to us.

And the deeper the love, the deeper the grief, it seems.

Have you ever sat in a room full of family members and just stared at them? Have you analyzed them until they became almost unrecognizable? Have you ever thought, *wow, what did it take for us to be here, together, right now? Why has God chosen these specific people to be my family members?* Or even more profound questions, like, *what is inside of them that I desperately need? What about them will help me see, understand, or experience life from the perspective of my ultimate destiny? Why was I created to fly with this particular flock?*

I've got an answer: to shape us into the people we're supposed to be. Family shapes who we are. We can start with the obvious. We share the same DNA. There is a distinct identity within us that cannot be authentically duplicated, replaced, or undone. Our genetics cause us to share certain aspects of our anatomy, habits, and unique tendencies.

The familial relationships we develop and grow with those who share our DNA are so powerful because of the nature of our connection. These relationships teach us, prepare us, and groom us to handle every other type of relationship we encounter. They are the foundation on which we discover our roles and positions in life. We learn who and how to obey, trust, confide in, and receive counsel from. Without familial relationships, it's more difficult to understand some of life's most essential lessons: the beauty of time and seasons, and the power of vulnerability.

Our values and standards often stem from what we're taught in our younger years. Whether positive or negative, occurrences within the family unit teach us valuable lessons and principles that stick with us for the rest of our lives.

One principle my parents instilled in me was to believe in myself. They told me that whatever dream I put effort into would eventually be successful if I worked hard and faithfully. I appreciate my parents for constantly reminding me of such principles— otherwise, I would have given up on many more things in life.

Without these principles, I would have lived unaware of the will-power and inner strength I possessed enough to finish a great deal of things I've started, especially on my darkest days when I felt like giving up entirely.

Then there are lessons that you have to discover on your own. You know, the consequential lessons that come along with dis-obeying your parents? When they tell you not to do something, and you do it anyway, only to find out that they were right and that you could have saved yourself the trauma if only you lis-tened and obeyed in the first place?

These types of lessons often stick for a lot longer. Life lessons that emerge from the home environment could easily translate into the outside world. What we learn in our younger years can prepare us for how we handle experiences later on in life. The log-ic behind how we choose to handle certain situations through-out life can be heavily influenced by those we are surrounded by the most—and for most of us, that's family.

THE BEAUTIFUL AND HARSH REALITIES OF TIME AND SEASON

"I remember the day you were born."

"I remember when you were this small."

"Where has the time gone!"

I'm sure you've heard at least one of these phrases in your life-time. Maybe you haven't seen Uncle Richard in years, and finally, at the family barbeque, he is surprised to see that his baby niece or nephew has grown into an adult. There's also a little twinkle in his eye. Do you want to know what that twinkle is?

It's the disbelief of time's passing.

He's trying to wrap his head around how he's allowed so much time to pass since the last time he's seen you. He's overwhelmed by the fact that he's practically missed most of your human development.

Since becoming an aunt, I have to admit that I've been on the front end of these "twinkle-eyed" moments. I freak out if I don't see my niece or nephews for over two weeks. They've learned new words, they're an inch longer or taller than our last hangout, or they pick up a new habit I've never seen before. Every time this happens, my eyes twinkle in disbelief and excitement that these humans before me, once peanuts, have wonderfully developed into older, more mature versions of themselves.

Moments like these should prompt us to step back and examine *how* we spend our time, who we invest it in, and whether the ways we've chosen to spend our time have been worth it. Family is the group of people we get the privilege to see grow through almost every life stage and season. My obsession and love for my family has made me more sensitive to the beauty of time.

The beauty of sitting in a park picnicking with them on summer afternoons or cheering for our favorite sports teams during playoff seasons in the comfort of one of our homes. However family time goes, I'm always left with peace, knowing our time was well-spent because we're together. Nothing's better than that.

Understanding how precious time spent with family is makes us better stewards of our time.

A TIME TO REFLECT

Think about the number of hours we allocate to work, dreams, chores or errands, extra-curricular hobbies, and leisure activities per week. How would you prioritize the following responsibilities? List your order by placing a 1-5 beside each category below:

Work

_____

_____

_____

Dreams

_____

_____

_____

Chores/errands

_____

_____

_____

Extra-curricular hobbies

_____

_____

_____

Leisure activities

_____

_____

_____

Where would you rank family amongst these categories? With the understanding that not all family dynamics are the same, I'm confident that most of us who follow through with this exercise will have rated family the highest. It's no secret. We are relational beings with the desire to connect, and the blessing of family is often our first touchpoint of genuine connection.

It is when we lose close connections that we come to understand the blessing of them fully. When I lost my mother, everything I deemed more important than spending time with her while she was alive suddenly became meaningless. There was no friend night out, soccer game, or life dream that could weigh in comparison to how rich of a moment sitting down with Mom over a cup of tea would have or could have been. Now, every moment I can savour with a loved one counts.

Take advantage of the time you have and the position you are in now before it's too late.

Spending time with those we love produces trust and vulnerability. In most cases, our families are the people who get to experience the most vulnerable parts of us.

After a full day of facing the real world, we go home to a place of familiarity where we can walk, talk, and live freely. For some of us, our family members are our listening ears, the people with whom we can share our deepest thoughts, worries, wins, and breakthroughs. They have the backstage pass to the authentic, raw, unedited versions of us.

Maybe your family members are your best friends. That's fine, too.

The point is that we all have people in our lives with whom we are comfortable being our complete selves—and we need them. It is with these people that we can express some of our deepest emotions.

Vulnerability is like a good old detox. The human body needs a full detox to reset its systems every now and again. Similarly, our souls need a healthy, vulnerable release every now and again—a time to release any thoughts, feelings, and emotions that may be bottled up inside our brains or our hearts.

Society's social standards would tell us differently, encouraging us to suppress our emotions in an effort to make others comfortable.

I remember the days I'd take GO Train trips Westbound to Union Station in Toronto. On morning express trains with hundreds of people resembling packed sardines in a tin can, you could hear the sound of a pin drop—if you take away the sound of the train rushing through on the tracks. The operator would announce, "Attention riders. Just a reminder that the quiet zone is in effect for this express train." If you coughed, accidentally triggered a morning playlist aloud, or briefly greeted an old friend you haven't seen in a while, tons of eyes would pierce in your direction as if to suggest that you shut up—and quickly. Or jump off of the train while it was still at full speed.

Living in a society like this causes us to shy away from being expressive. It actually encourages us to shrink in a sense. That's why it's so important to appreciate the safe spaces we have and the people who dwell there.

That's family. They're where you'll find a shoulder to lean on when the going gets tough. They allow us to feel a sense of belonging and trust in the world.

I experienced my share of rejection in my adolescent and teenage years. I was rejected because of the colour of my skin, my beliefs, and my ease in embracing my uniqueness. I was excluded from opportunities I passionately chased after, had decisions made for me without the opportunity to give my own input, and was constantly talked about behind my back. Home was where I was able to explore my truest thoughts and feelings about such rejection.

If not for a space to lay my head and air out my grievances, worries, and frustrations.

If not for a space to fully express endless feelings through words, anger, or tears.

If not for the precious gift of vulnerability with the people I love and who know me best.

Choosing to be vulnerable is like taking a courageous journey into the heart of who we truly are. It's like peeling back the layers of our story, uncovering the raw and authentic parts of ourselves that make us uniquely human. This self-discovery deepens our understanding of ourselves and acts as a bridge, connecting us more intimately with the people around us. When we allow ourselves to be vulnerable, we create a space for genuine connections to flourish. It's like inviting others to join us on this adventure of self-discovery, sharing our triumphs and our weaknesses. In doing so, we strengthen the bonds that tie us together, weaving a tapestry of relationships rich in authenticity and mutual understanding.

Vulnerability is powerful. And vulnerability can only be exercised in the company of a trusted flock. Do you have one?

When a flock of birds paint the sky in synchronicity, you'll rarely find a single bird taking its own path, but it's possible, and for so many different reasons. Maybe this wayward bird is injured or old and unable to fly as it used to.

Isn't that life, though? Sometimes, the inevitable tendencies of a mortal life can slow us down or prevent us from living as we once knew it.

My mother slowly faded from our family flock as she bravely battled lung cancer. While watching her fight, I often wondered how it might have felt to live with the thought of saying goodbye to us, her family, while still holding out on faith that she would make it through her storm. It wasn't until listening to the unexpected audible gift of her journey with God that I actually got a taste of what that might have felt like for her.

In the recording, while being pulled into a supernatural flight with God, she said, "But what about my family?" Interestingly, my mother's first thought was to inquire about us—her family. Her flock. But why?

I'd like to think that her immediate call for us attests to the one-of-a-kind connectivity she felt with us—what most of us experience with family members. That wholeness rests in our souls whenever those we love are intimately near. Even though Mom didn't pass away until a month after her miraculous journey with Jesus, I sense it was during this particular moment when she uttered the words, "But what about my family? Goodbye, family," that she peacefully resolved to part from us.

Mom sensed that where she was going was worth the cost of losing what was the most valuable to her on earth. She was willing to pay that price. And paying the price isn't all that easy.

Sometimes, the things we want and need conflict with each other. Mom wanted to spend more time with us on earth, yet she craved to be swept away to heavenly places by the God she had known and served all her years. It must have been frightening and thrilling to be so torn between those two realities.

A TIME TO REFLECT

1. Think about it: Who's a part of your flock? Who are the first people that come to mind?

_____

_____

_____

_____

_____

2. Let's dig deeper. List 5-10 people you know who have helped you exercise true vulnerability. Don't be intimidated or overwhelmed by this exercise. No flock is too big or too small.

_____

_____

_____

_____

_____

Your Life, Your Choice

4

O n multiple occasions, I've heard people say that they're mad at God because they believed He had done something to deliberately disappoint them.

Can I tell you what I believe?

These people are half right. I believe that the pain and disappointment we encounter in life can be deliberate, but I also believe that the overall intent of that pain and disappointment is not to ruin your life.

Yet, I also believe God intended for our lives to be perfect, without spots or wrinkles. No pain. No suffering. No loss. No death. No failure. No mistakes.

But then came this thing called sin, and because of its onset from the beginning in Genesis, we are left to deal with its realities, effects, and consequences as long as we dwell here on planet Earth. It's like a sloppy packaged deal. God does not send pain and disappointment to us. He just allows them to encounter us.

Why would God allow pain and disappointment to encounter us?

Well, that's just it—so that we would turn to Him and ask Him questions.

Sometimes, the problematic situations in our lives position our hearts to welcome helpful life lessons from the Creator, the One who knew, from the beginning, when and how we'd eventually reach our breaking points.

The beautiful reality is that in all of our wondering, pleading, and questioning, He is right there, longing to pour into us and spend time with us in the middle of it all. All He requires of us is our time and our hearts, as broken or weak as they may be. In return, He promises his protection and presence.

When we lean into God, He shares His heart concerning our trials, with us. He offers us spiritual insight and tunes our desires and expectations into alignment with His will. When we do life with God, our difficulties are never for nothing. They don't exist in our lives just to make us miserable.

When we do life with God, we can rest in the fact that our difficulties are purposeful and directional, meaning that God has a specific purpose and place for that small, "ugly" piece of your life puzzle.

***

I received the revelation to write this book over ten years ago. You can call procrastination my kryptonite, but writing in my personal journal is much less intimidating than writing for the world.

Writing this book meant revisiting the broken parts of me, putting them into words, and publicizing them. It meant reliving my darkest moments and uncovering unhealed wounds repeatedly. So I waited. I pondered back and forth in my head for years about whether I would go through with writing this book or hoard this information and keep it all to myself.

Reasoning between these two decisions was exhausting.

Until one day, something inside of me came alive. After a full workday on November 17, 2016, I rushed home with the sudden desire to hear my mother's voice again. I went digging in my room to find my voice recorder and replayed that 18-minute first-class journey while smiling ear-to-ear, with soft and slow tears running down my face. By this point, listening to this special recording was a quarterly habit of mine. I often listened to keep this life-defining memory fresh, but things felt different this time.

While listening to that recording, I was moved to pen some ideas that later turned into the theme and chapters of the book you are now holding.

I'd felt the push to pursue writing a book many times before this moment. I'm confident that God nudged, poked, and whispered in my ear more times than He probably wanted to. I believe I heard Him encourage me to spend more time with Him and start brainstorming how I would share my experiences with the world, but I ignored it.

On that November evening, I finally listened, and something miraculous happened.

Here's my journal entry from that day:

November 17, 2016

"When we submit to God's plans, He grants us the desires of our hearts—sometimes even the desires we didn't realize we longed for the most."

'Delight yourself in the Lord, and he will give you the desires of your heart.' Psalm 37:4 [ESV]

Tonight was a night I will never, ever forget. I came home with a sudden urge to start writing. I've been praying about writing and what to do with this love of mine, but my hand was too heavy to pick up a pen. Or at least that's what I convinced myself. I wanted to write, but I just didn't DO it. I know that God wants me to write. I know that there is a specific task that He's called me to fulfill. He wants to birth something inside of me. I just need to trust Him. I just need to let Him.

So today, I grabbed my voice recorder, which still had my mother's journey on it after six years, and I pressed play. Various ideas for chap-

ter themes and titles burst out of me. The recording spoke to me in ways I've never experienced before. It was amazing. After hours of working in my element, I stopped writing. I felt like I had given all of myself to this very moment. Everything I wrote came from what was stored within me after all these years. I was satisfied to release it.

Just when I thought my quiet night of writing was over, my father entered my room. He didn't knock.

"I've never sat on your bed since we moved here," he said.

We had lived in our new home for over two years. We talked about our days and how busy life had been. Soon after, our conversation transitioned back to my mother's recording. We talked about how much we missed her, how special she was, and how much of a blessing she had been to our lives. We talked about her legacy and the sweet aroma she left with everyone she met.

At that moment, I noticed my dad's eyes had become red. Tears fell as he spoke about the wonderful woman he knew Mom to be. This quickly became my fondest memory with my father. The quote I wrote at the beginning of this entry is dear to my heart because I realized that the moment I submitted myself to God by pinning myself down to start this book, this beautiful moment with Daddy occurred. This moment mended parts of me I didn't even know were broken. So I guess I want to say sorry, God, for not listening to you immediately. I could have experienced this feeling of peace and joy sooner had I listened to your Word. I love you. So much."

Caroline

I shared this journal entry with the intent to ask you two specific questions.

Question 1: What will you turn your attention to?

Is there a calling you've been ignoring? Are you allowing brokenness, lack of confidence, confusion, or anxiety to discourage you from doing that thing even though you know deep down in your heart that it's a genuine desire, affirmed and stamped with approval by the One who planted it inside of you? Will you continue to hold this God-given desire hostage, or will you say yes to positioning yourself for action? Will you commit to spending time with God, asking Him what to do next, and sitting still in His presence until He speaks? Will you turn your attention to Him so He can show you the way forward? I hope you say yes to all of that.

Question 2: What will you do with what God allows you to encounter?

How will you respond to the trials you are dealt? Will you think of them as punishment and dare to hate God? Will you choose to remain in the place of disappointment indefinitely? Or, will you firmly hold your negative thoughts and emotions captive, all the while trusting that even in the yet undiscovered or unfelt aspects, your pain has a purposeful place to land? Will you believe that God knows all and sees all and that He sees far enough to know that you will one day make it through your hurt and struggle? Will you trust that He is good enough to lead you out of darkness and into His marvellous Light?

I could have allowed my mother's death to put me in an everlasting depression, but I chose to find the hidden treasure that lay amongst the dirt and rubble of my situation.

This wasn't easy, though. The weight of grief felt insurmountable, and the healing journey seemed like an endless, daunting road. It took considerable time—years— to traverse the shadows of despair and find solace in the Light again. In those moments of profound darkness, where hope seemed elusive, the presence of Jesus gradually illuminated my path. It wasn't an overnight transformation; healing from such profound loss is gradual.

Through prayer and built-up faith, I discovered a resilience I never knew I possessed. Jesus became a source of solace, guiding me through the waves of grief and pointing me toward a renewed sense of purpose. It took time and patience, but the possibility of overcoming the shadows became increasingly tangible with each step taken in faith. In embracing Jesus' love, I found the courage to confront my grief, first through writing. I allowed God to guide my healing process, and He allowed this process to unfold at its own pace.

Today, I stand on the other side of that darkness, not untouched by the pain but strengthened by the unwavering presence of a Savior who walked with me through every step of my grief journey.

The choice to heal from loss is not easy, but it is always your choice. And it's a choice you'll have to make every single day.

My best choice was to let God in and listen to His direction as best I could. In time, He led me to a beautiful place. I hope you let Him in, too.

A TIME TO REFLECT

1. What is one choice you need to make today concerning a situation you are currently facing?

   _____

   _____

   _____

   _____

2. What can you do to sustain your commitment to this choice?

   _____

   _____

   _____

   _____

Oh, To Be Selfless

5

'll never forget the day my elementary class watched the movie "Pay It Forward." I'll never forget how this movie made me feel, even as a young adolescent. Released in 2000, this drama-romance, based on a novel of the same title by Catherine Ryan Hyde, tells the story of a young 12-year-old boy. His school teacher challenges him to devise a creative idea to change the world. The boy decides to help three people in unique ways, then encourages them to help three more people, and so forth—a domino effect, if you will. The boy's mother is greatly moved by her son's commitment to positively impact the lives of others through the following gestures: talking a woman off of a bridge, literally welcoming a homeless man into their home, and starting a powerful movement of giving and kindness.

I felt so many emotions when leaving the classroom that day. On one hand, I felt inspired to carry the baton of kindness to every person I'd come in contact with from that point on. On the other hand, I felt conflicted, unable to identify what I'd be willing to give up to serve the people in my world. I asked myself: *To what extent am I willing to put myself out there, get out of my comfort zone, and be brave for the benefit of another human being? What made these people pay it forward, anyway?*

THE POWER OF SELFLESSNESS

Selflessness is the ability to care for the needs and wants of others over your own. Humanity, as a whole, could focus more on being selfless. One act of selflessness could awaken a sense of belonging and acceptedness in a world that screams, "You're on your own!"

Selflessness can be as big as missing an important meeting to be emotional support for a close friend or as small as paying for the order behind you in a fast-food restaurant drive-thru. What's important is that you put yourself, your desires, your fears, and even your comfort to the side for the benefit of another.

Over the years, I've learned that selflessness can leave you in two separate places. You feel the inner peace to go the extra mile for the benefit of another, or a greater good (place one), but, you might also have to lay your desires down and trust that your selflessness will at some point bear fruit, even if you don't feel all that sweet (place two).

There's a fascinating story in the Bible about two men who taught me a lot about the power of selflessness and the unexpected blessings that can arise from our willingness to be selfless. An uncle and nephew travelled extensively until they finally settled on the land they were assigned to bring their families and livestock. Still, since the uncle and the nephew had several possessions, the land they settled on was not large enough to support them both.

There was a massive dispute between both families until the uncle finally allowed his nephew to choose any section of the land he wanted. He (the uncle) would then settle elsewhere. The nephew chose the beautiful, flourishing, and well-watered portion of land to the East of them for his family and livestock. And so, the uncle accepted the remaining unfavourable land for his livestock—poor uncle.

Or so we thought.

After settling in the abundant land, the nephew discovered that people had already lived there. They were very nasty and troublesome toward him and his family. On the other hand, his uncle had settled in what later became an abundance of good land with much more space than he had expected. The uncle received confirmation that the land he settled on was his, and his livestock's, forever. This land reached farther than his eyes could see—in each direction. Wow.

This is the famous bible story of Abram (the uncle) and Lot (the nephew), derived from Genesis 13.

In this story, Abram selflessly offers Lot the first land choice to end a dispute. Lot chose the better-looking section of the land; it was pleasing to the eye. In the end, he was fooled. Lot and his family had to cope with his hasty and haughty decision, while Abram, the selfless, calm, cool, and collected man who carried no worry in his heart, ended up with the most beautiful land—more than he could ever ask for. The land of Canaan.

Upon settling in Canaan, Abram's new dwelling place, God speaks to Abram in Genesis 13:17 (NKJV), saying, *"Arise, walk in the land through its length and its width, for I give it to you."*

Abram settled in the land that had already been given to him. God settled it before Abram settled. It was destiny. He didn't have to bicker and fuss about anything with his nephew to get what he wanted. Instead, he surrendered, and he was selfless. Through a simple act of selflessness, Abram proved his trust in the Lord's leading and the Lord's ultimate will for his life.

Through this Bible story, I've learned that entrusting my life to God's guidance, much like Abram, can be enlightening. It teaches on the profound importance of relinquishing control and surrendering my decisions to His wisdom. There's an inherent vulnerability in admitting that my understanding might be limited and that my choices, however well-intentioned, may not always align with what's best for me.

It's a delicate dance between the desire for autonomy and the recognition that the Lord's wisdom surpasses my finite understanding. There have been instances where I, in my limited perspective, have made decisions that seemed right at the time but later unfolded into unforeseen challenges. The significance of surrendering control to God becomes glaringly apparent during these moments.

Guarding against the impulse to rely solely on my understanding (Proverbs 3:5-6), I've learned to lean on God's guidance for discernment. It's all about acknowledging that His perspective transcends the constraints of my human comprehension. While the world urges self-reliance, the beauty lies in recognizing that true empowerment often comes from accepting our limitations and placing trust in God.

Relinquishing control does not imply passivity; rather, inviting the Lord's guidance into our decision-making processes is an active choice. It's about aligning our will with God's, understanding that His plans may differ from our own but are ultimately designed for our well-being. Through this surrender, we can discover a peace that emanates from knowing we're not navigating life's complexities alone.

I'd like to believe that there was a point in my mother's cancer journey, likely after her Acceptance stage, that she realized her only way to get through this life challenge was to understand that she didn't have the final say. She had to learn and understand that only God had the final say.

It's often hard for us to come to that resolution. We like to believe that since *we* are the *only* ones living *our* lives, it's only fitting that we have a say—dare I say the final say—concerning our lives.

We're like babies who can't walk yet but think, at just one month old, that it's about time we start walking down a set of wooden stairs. Our parents, who know better, rescue us from taking that deathly first step. Out of frustration, we kick and scream as they hold us tight in their arms. We have no idea what our parents saved us from.

It's later in life, when our maturity kicks in, that we understand the purpose of the restrictions once set before us. We realize that our parents actually knew better than we did, and we can trust that their restrictions for us were for our benefit. When we grow in wisdom and understanding, we are less resistant to letting our parents lead us in the right direction.

The same goes for how we trust God with our lives. With maturity, it becomes increasingly logical to trust His will for our lives and every single step that gets us there.

There was a time during my mother's first-class journey when she displayed her willingness to relinquish control to God concerning her time left on earth, and in this surrender, she also displayed a degree of selflessness.

THE RELINQUISHING OF CONTROL

In recounting this journey, Mom remembered saying, "Bye, family," immediately implying that wherever God was taking her was where she needed to be.

She didn't have to think much. Her immediate response was "bye." What trust she had to go willingly.

What faith she had in Jesus.

She also said, "I should have just gone [with Jesus for a little while] and told Him I wanted to come back [to earth] after experiencing time with Him."

Now, I know that doesn't sound selfless at all. It sounds a lot more *selfish*. Mom was trying to get the best of both worlds—where on earth does that happen?

Ultimately, my mother did the total *opposite* of what she said she should have done. She didn't ask for a quick trip to the anticipated unknown and then ask to be brought back to the people she loved. She inquired about us. She asked to say goodbye. She cared for us so much that she couldn't help but worry about what life would have been like for us without her. And as an act of true love, she momentarily sacrificed something significant to her. She risked forfeiting her first-class, one-way trip with the Lord, just to see her tribe.

When we relinquish control to God, we leave room to seek His heart's desire for us and others. We are coated with a layer of compassion. We can see how fiercely loved we are by God, and we can rest in the fact that He would never lead us astray, but instead, lead us right on track to His will for us.

A TIME TO REFLECT

1. What is one thing you need to relinquish control over and give completely to God?

_____

_____

_____

_____

2. What is one selfless act you can pay forward today?

_____

_____

_____

_____

Faith—God's Love Language

6

Sometimes, the positive outcome of our faith is immediately evident.

I recall a time when my faith produced instant results. After a full workday, I was headed to an evening class in Toronto. Evening parking in the lot nearest to my destination was six dollars. I was in a rush to make it to class on time, and I didn't think I had enough change to pay this amount in cash, which was the only accepted payment method for this particular lot.

Stopping at the bank was a strain, as it meant I'd be late for yet another class—something I wasn't proud of. I was out of options. Desperation had me searching my wallet for six dollars in change (which I already knew I didn't have—or so I thought). The simple act of digging into my wallet for change was a leap of faith because I rarely kept cash in my wallet.

To my surprise, I found $3.75 in my wallet. Pretty impressive, but still not enough to pay for parking. I was then compelled to check a small compartment in my car where I would sometimes store loose change—another subconscious faith move.

Can I tell you how freaked out I was when I found the exact amount of change I needed?

Whew.

It's occurrences like these that build up my faith. Looking back on this experience, I now see how scurrying for change to secure a parking spot can resemble a griever's journey.

My journey. Our journey.

Each coin represents a fragment of solace, a glimmer of hope desperately needed to carry on. Amidst profound loss, it can feel as though we're frantically searching for these tiny tokens of comfort to sustain us through the storm.

With every coin discovered, there's a fleeting moment of relief, a brief respite from the weight of sorrow. In these moments, we find the strength to keep going and press forward despite the ache in our hearts. Yet we're often left wondering if these small comforts will ever be enough to see us through.

But then something remarkable happens. As we continue to gather these coins of solace, they accumulate one by one, day by day. What once sustained us for a moment now builds into something more substantial. These coins—these sustained moments of solace—gradually evolve into days, weeks, months, and eventually, years.

In time, we realize that the coins we've gathered along the way have formed a foundation of resilience. What initially seemed like a futile endeavour has transformed into a testament to our ability to endure and overcome. Each coin represents a moment of healing, a step forward on the path toward wholeness.

Through the journey of grief, we learn to trust in the healing process. We discover that even in the darkest moments, there is always a glimmer of light to guide us forward. And as we continue to dig for those coins of solace, we find that they become the currency of our resilience, sustaining us through the most challenging of times.

So, my friend, as you grieve, keep digging.

***

I'm sure you've heard the fictional tale of *The Little Engine*

That Could.[6]

To me, this is a famous story that also focuses on the power and purpose of faith in one's life.

In a nutshell, *The Little Engine That Could* is a story about a jolly little train on its way to deliver toys for children on the other side of a great mountain. When the train approaches the foot of the mountain, its engine breaks down, leaving it to sit still at the foot of the mountain, which delays the delivery of toys to the children. The little train of cars remains hopeful that another engine will soon pass by to help it up to the mountain. Eventually, a great, robust, shiny engine passes by but refuses to help because it is too prideful and thinks that the little train of cars is too worthless to pull along. A small old and rusty engine also passes by, but it is too weak to pull the little train of toys, saying, "I never could, I never could." Finally, after a long, long time, there comes a little small engine. It is cheerful and happy. Although it seemed ridiculous to ask such a little engine to pull such a loaded train of cars, the little train of cars begs for assistance. The Little Engine is delighted and determined to help pull the toys to the other side of the mountain. At first, The Little Engine struggles, but with time, it starts gaining momentum, steadily tracking up to the mountain. Further along the way, The Little Engine begins puffing, yet still encourages *itself* to keep pushing towards the top of the mountain, saying, "I think I can, I think I can!" Eventually, The Little Engine makes it to the top of the mountain! And so, the children on the other side of the mountain received their toys with glee.

The moral of the story: don't count yourself out. You are unstoppable—if only you would have faith, try your best, and believe!

---

6 Piper, Watty. *The Little Engine That Could.* Illustrated by George and Doris Hauman, Platt & Munk, 1930.

Children's stories like *The Little Engine That Could* have a funny way of highlighting Biblical truths:

"NOW FAITH is the substance of things hoped for, the evidence of things not seen." Hebrews 11:1 KJV, *emphasis added*

Whether or not you know this scripture, I'm almost sure that you've heard this truth in phrases like, "Believe it 'till you see it," or, "Fake it 'till you make it." Either way, I believe that in the practical sense, Hebrews 11:1 is saying that faith is the unshakable belief in something or someone that you have yet to see or experience. The Little Engine couldn't see the other side of the mountain while struggling to get there, but by faith, it hoped and believed for the strength to get there.

LOUD FAITH: THE POWERFUL PAIR OF BELIEF AND ACTION

Between the story of *The Little Engine That Could* and my six-dollar parking story, there is one underlying truth I'd like to draw out: the power of speaking aloud and declaring a thing.

While searching for change to reach my six-dollar target, I kept saying to myself, "C'mon, I'm almost there, just 50, 20, 10 more cents." Believe it or not, that was an act of faith. We can compare this to The Little Engine's declaration, "I think I can, I think I can!"

Would things have turned out the same if I or The Little Engine had said nothing? Would we have kept going? I personally think not. I think our silence would breed defeat, inaction, and stagnancy. Living a faith-driven life isn't always easy and smooth sailing. Sometimes, the desired result of our faith takes a little longer to materialize than we expect or want it to.

You might think I'm crazy to say this, but I believe that delayed gratification—waiting—is quite possibly the best thing that could ever happen to our faith.

Waiting strengthens our faith and grooms us to exercise positive hopefulness in times of hopelessness.

> WAITING STRENGTHENS OUR FAITH AND GROOMS US TO EXERCISE POSITIVE HOPEFULNESS IN TIMES OF HOPELESSNESS.

So, if faith grows when its outcome is delayed, what do you do in the meantime? Here are three things I've learned that faith requires of us before we can see what we seek after:

1. FAITH REQUIRES YOU TO BELIEVE.

To honestly believe in something is to have no doubt. To believe in something is to speak positively concerning it. It's to encourage. Encouragement is like a good cup of coffee or an energy drink. It's most effective when consistent.

The Little Engine That Could had faith to believe they could make it up the mountain. While huffing and puffing up the mountain with all its might, it repeatedly encouraged itself, saying, "I think I can, I think I can" until it conquered the mountain.

While scrambling in the crevices of my car, dollars short of my six-dollar parking expense, I had faith that the change I needed was available to me and repeatedly encouraged myself to keep searching for it.

It's vital to have the faith to believe in any situation, especially when things aren't yet where you want them to be. That's the only way up and out.

But don't be fooled, my friend; encouraging yourself—though it sounds awesome and empowering—isn't always smooth sailing. There will be days that speaking life into yourself comes easy, where you can say, "You can do hard things," but there may also be days you will only have the strength to say, "You can."

Whenever you can, however you can, and in whatever situation you find yourself in, do your best to conjure up as much faith as you can to believe and encourage yourself.

Huff and puff until you get to the other side.

Search and scramble until you have enough change.

Do whatever it takes to keep believing.

2. FAITH REQUIRES YOU TO OPEN YOUR MOUTH.

Something significant happens when we back our faith up with a verbal commitment and declaration. Think about it: before two individuals are officially declared husband and wife at their wedding, they must publicly and verbally declare their vows and seal them with an "I do."

Now, let's picture the total opposite scenario. Imagine facing your betrothed at the altar on your wedding day. The wedding officiant asks them, "Do you take this man or woman to be your lawfully wedded husband or wife?" They barely respond with a shrug, or a tinge better, a nod—and not a word comes out of their mouth.

How much faith would you have in your supposed union after witnessing such an underwhelming response from the one you love? How assured would you feel in moving forward with this marriage? Probably not so much.

I'd imagine any person getting married to the love of their life would want to have sure faith in the longevity of their union. They'd want to hear their partner publicly declare their love and commitment to a lifelong relationship with the utmost poise and passion. To conceive such a faith, someone would *have* to open their mouth.

Or what about confirmation ceremonies that are held for public leaders, prime ministers, presidents, kings, and queens? Do they hold their hand to a Bible, nod their heads, and remain silent while accepting a laundry list of responsibilities offloaded to them as distinct members of society? No—how much faith do you reckon a country or nation would have in this leader if this was the case? Instead, they are expected to declare their commitment to leadership vocally.

There's also the story of the two blind men who were miraculously healed by Jesus in Matthew 9:27-29. Let's read it together:

"As Jesus went on from there, two blind men followed him, calling out, 'Have mercy on us, Son of David!' When he had gone indoors, the blind men came to him, and he asked them, 'Do you believe that I am able to do this?' 'Yes, Lord,' they replied. Then he touched their eyes and said, 'According to your faith let it be done to you.' "

Jesus knew that He could heal them, but He asked the blind men if they believed in His power to heal them. He wanted to know for certain that they believed. And to prove and confirm their belief in Him, they had to open their mouths and declare, "Yes, Lord."

Opening our mouths gives us the courage to keep on keeping on.

I doubt I, or the Engine, would have continued for as long as we did if we didn't hear our *own* voices spewing out Faith Gatorade from the sidelines as we sprinted to our respective finish lines with all of the strength we had left.

3. FAITH REQUIRES YOU TO MOVE.

"Even so faith, if it hath not works, is dead, being alone."
–James 2:17, KJV

It's one thing to believe in something with all your might, but it's another thing to accompany your belief with action.

Always apply action.

Step back in time to the ancient lands of Judea, where stories of miracles and divine intervention were woven into the fabric of everyday life. Among these tales, one stands out as a testament to the power of faith and the boundless mercy of God: the resurrection of Lazarus.

In the gospel of John, we encounter a poignant narrative that unfolds in the small village of Bethany, where Lazarus, a dear friend of Jesus, falls gravely ill. As his sisters, Mary and Martha, watch over him with bated breath, they send word to Jesus, their beloved teacher and healer, pleading for his intervention.

What follows is a remarkable sequence of events that defies human understanding and reveals the profound depths of Jesus' love for his friends.

"...Jesus called in a loud voice, 'Lazarus, come out!' The dead man came out, his hands and feet wrapped with strips of linen, and a cloth around his face. Jesus said to them, 'Take off the grave clothes and let him go' " (John 11:43-44, NIV).

Bear with me and my theatrical mind for a second.

When Jesus called Lazarus, he was still wrapped in linen (a super strong fabric that can not easily be broken out of). When he heard Jesus call him saying, "Come out," I wonder if he was discouraged at first, thinking, "I can't move. I'm wrapped up in all this linen."

Perhaps amidst his wrapped-up state, he found the faith and courage to move—with the help of his sisters, of course. Sure, it would have been tough for him to walk to his freedom, but perhaps he shimmied, wabbled, or rolled. He did whatever it took to get to Jesus.

Lazarus moved. Movement was key. Sometimes you just have to move.

In the realm of faith, actions speak volumes. It's not just about what we say we believe; it's about how we live out those beliefs in our everyday lives. Taking action to prove our faith is like putting our money where our mouth is—it's about walking the walk, not just talking the talk.

Think about it like this: Faith without action is like a car without gas—it might look good, but it's not going anywhere. That's why you'll often hear people say that faith without works is dead.

When we act to prove our faith, we're not just making a statement; we're making a difference. Whether we lend a helping hand to someone in need, stand up for what's right, or spread kindness wherever we go, our actions can change lives—for ourselves and others.

> WHEN WE ACT TO PROVE OUR FAITH, WE'RE NOT JUST MAKING A STATEMENT; WE'RE MAKING A DIFFERENCE.

And here's the cool part: when we act to prove our faith, we're not doing it alone. We're partnering up with Jesus, trusting that He's got our back every step of the way.

FAITH IN THE UNPOPULAR PACKAGE

Sometimes, the outcome of our faith doesn't come in the package we expect.

"I believe I'm healed."

My mother said this with unwavering faith at the near end of explaining her first-class journey. She said it with so much passion. The tone of her voice inspired me to believe in her healing with every fibre of my being. I cried real tears at that very moment. If my faith was the juice of a lemon, I had squeezed out every last drop.

But she wasn't physically healed in the end.

This unmet expectation shook the entire foundation of my Christian faith. I questioned God for days. Weeks. Months. Years.

How could this be?

I had prayed my most radical prayers, I read ample scripture, and our family banded together to support each other every single day. We did the best we could to make Mom laugh as much as possible. But did anything we tried even take effect?

I questioned God.

Do you even hear me when I call out to You?

Are You listening to me at all?

Hello? I'm right here.

Why are You ignoring me?

Are You even real?

Have I been believing in You falsely this entire time?

And one more thing. Why?

These were my rawest thoughts and feelings. I battled with disappointment, failure, and guilt the entire time I'd witnessed her deteriorating before my very eyes.

I was bitter. Numb.

That was until the day I was suddenly hit with another thought: my mother was so calm and peaceful as she shared her assurance for healing in her first-class journey. For someone who was at the time facing a terminal illness, she wore a crown of peace so elegantly, unlike anyone I had ever seen.

But how?

Well, I believe she had already claimed her healing.

Her healing hadn't occurred physically as we had expected. Her healing took place in the spiritual realm.

And isn't that how God is?

Sometimes, He answers us in the ways we least expect, even in ways we *think* we don't want Him to. Faith kept my mother sane amidst uncertainty, doubt, and confusion. Through this, I learned that one's ability to apply their faith in trying times is entirely up to themselves.

> SOMETIMES, HE ANSWERS US IN THE WAYS WE LEAST EXPECT, EVEN IN WAYS WE *THINK* WE DON'T WANT HIM TO.

So, how do you exercise your faith when you don't get what you pray for?

Remember when I said that, in a practical sense, faith is the unshakable belief in something or someone you haven't seen yet? Well, as simple as that beautiful definition might seem, faith, in reality, is not as easy to live out.

Faith is risky; you never really know the outcome, but you know what you want it to be. And even if you don't get the outcome you want, there's this thing that, through and by faith, can hold you firmly together even when you feel like everything around you is falling apart.

It's called contentment.

CONTENTMENT

One night, I was driving a young friend home after a midweek Bible study service at my church.

"So, what's been going on, girly? How was your day?" I asked.

"Honestly, my day was horrible."

"Horrible? Oh no, how come?" I asked.

"I don't know, I've just been discontent," she said.

Oh boy, here comes another deep convo. I had to plead for the Holy Spirit's guidance. After a few moments of internal pleading, the Lord filled my mouth with this simple question:

"What is the source of your contentment?"

The young lady replied, "The source of my contentment comes from doing the things I love to do."

Then I hit her with another question:

"Where does God sit in all of this?"

"I don't know," she replied.

"So, if your contentment comes from doing the things you love, why are you discontent today?" I asked.

She replied, "Well, because I didn't have the time to do what I love today. I had other things to do. And some days, I'm just not feeling it."

Then it dawned on me. She wasn't talking about contentment; she was talking about *happiness*. Happiness is an emotional state that can change in a moment and is dependent on people, things, and occurrences.

Contentment is in a whole other ballpark of its own.

Contentment is a continual state of being. It cannot be shaken or moved. Contentment says, "No matter what," especially in times of crisis.

On that car ride home, I told the young lady that although I understood the excitement and fulfillment that came from her interests, allowing that to be her overall source of contentment would bring endless disappointment. Here's why.

The occurrence of those things was fleeting and inconsistent. My young friend said she didn't always have the time to do the things she loved because of other priorities. This leaves her feeling highly fulfilled on the days that she can carve out time for herself and empty on the days she has no time to engage in her favourite hobbies. See the pattern here?

I often imagine that my mother's cancer journey felt like sailing through inconsistent, stormy seas. Some days, you're riding the waves with ease, feeling happy and grateful for a smooth sail. But when the winds change, and the clouds roll in, finding that same sense of happiness can feel like trying to catch sunlight in a storm.

When life is going well, happiness comes naturally. It's easy to feel thankful and satisfied when everything's going your way. But when cancer enters the picture, maintaining that happiness can become a real challenge because you're constantly battling against fear, uncertainty, and physical discomfort, with each day bringing its own set of obstacles to overcome.

But here's the thing—amidst all the darkness, there are still moments of unexpected beauty and grace.

My mother's journey has led me to believe that finding *contentment*—rather than happiness—means shifting your perspective and embracing the present moment, no matter how difficult it may be. It's about finding solace in the small victories, cherishing moments of connection, and taking joy in the simple pleasures that life still has to offer.

Finding contentment doesn't mean pretending that everything's okay. It's about accepting challenges with courage and resilience while also recognizing the value of those struggles in shaping who we are and deepening our appreciation for life's precious moments and God's goodness.

Witnessing my mother's ability to be content while battling cancer was a testament to her strength, empowered only by the spirit of God. Hebrews 13:8 (NLT) says, *"Jesus Christ is the same yesterday and today and forever."*

Jesus Christ, the Son of God, is consistent. This is etched in His character and being. He never changes. God sent His Son to us so that we would accept Him as the anchor and foundation for our souls while living in an ever-changing, sinful, and deceitful world.

God is the source of our contentment. He holds the keys to everything that concerns us, including our joy, peace, and everything that is good. He also holds the keys to death, hell, and the grave. He controls the good and bad in our lives. The good remains good, and the bad becomes good because He makes all things good (Genesis 50:20, Mark 7:37). That is why He should be the source of our contentment. He is a consistent God with consistent results—the consistent results being that He shows us ourselves and how we're better off with Him than we are without Him. Circumstances that happen to us may affect our current moods, but they do not have the power to break us because, in the end, God is still holding us up with His consistent and victorious right hand.

To get to this peaceful place of contentment, you just need to be aware of God's rule and reign over your life. You must know His power and rely on His proven consistency. You have to trust that He has the keys to your destiny, come what may. You have to put all of your attention on Him.

I learned this while walking through my grief. I began this process thinking God was against me and that He didn't want what was best for me; otherwise, He would have spared my mother.

But he didn't.

I responded to this deep disappointment with, "How could you let this happen?" I asked God this question a million and one times and never really felt like I got a straightforward answer. I bet you could imagine just how frustrating that was.

But you know what I realized over time? I realized that I did get something. I got the consistency of God's comfort and peace.

Comfort, because no matter how frustrated I felt amidst my grief, my response was to turn to Him and ask Him questions—even though I wasn't certain I'd get an answer. I kept going to Him because He remained somewhat of a safe place, and I felt there was still but a glimmer of a chance that He would be able to hear me and someday provide an answer that would take my pain away, or at least lessen it.

I call this Pinky Hold Faith.

What's that you ask? It's the ability to hold on to your beliefs even if all roads don't seem to lead to that desired outcome. It's pressing into the little faith that you have left. It's to rely on what you know, in my case, prayer and digging into the Word of God, even when I felt so far from God.

To have a pinky hold on anything doesn't seem like much. In fact, it doesn't seem promising at all. But I've found a pinky hold to be as strong as a two-handed firm grip of a bodybuilder while lifting weights at a state champion competition. It's strong because it's an all-or-nothing type of grip. Everything's riding on this hold. This faith, though a Pinky Hold Faith, was enough to keep my attention on God when things in life became foggy.

Peace, because in time, there existed this internal stance within me that I couldn't quite put a name to. A stance that helped me temper my emotions, where in other cases, one would have lost all control.

Looking back, I believe this was the peace of God—not just any peace. This was God's peace, the peace that the Prince of Peace granted me and equipped me with to make it through anything. Even the loss of my mother.

But I didn't fully understand this type of peace or how to live with it—and neither did others. There were times when people would expect me to react a certain way amidst my grief journey that I just didn't, and this concerned them. It concerned me, too. That was until the Lord taught me that peace is less of a thing that I need to understand and more of a thing that I need to receive.

When I finally offloaded the pressure of trying to make sense of the peace God freely gave me, I was able to put more energy into living a more peaceful life—a life that expected hard times to come ever so often, but wouldn't be entirely derailed by them. In the midst of all of our questions and uncertainty, God promises His comfort and peace (Philippians 4:7). Would you receive it today?

As I said earlier, I interrogated God, asking, *how could you let this happen?* Yet, after realizing that amidst my disappointment, God's comfort and peace remained with me the entire time, this interrogation turned into a curious pursuit, flowing from a grateful heart.

I began to ask God, ever-so tenderly and with awe, *how could you consistently love me so well through this?*

After all of the times I blamed Him for the outcome of my mother's battle with cancer, He never left me. Instead, He sent His Holy Spirit to stay with me; to comfort me and to give me peace (John 14:26-27). I think God honoured the fact that even while frustrated and deviant, I chose to return to Him and demand Him for answers.

I think He saw that as a type of faith. I think He understood my constant coming back to Him as a type of unorthodox prayer for the season of life that I was in—and He was okay with that because it meant that I'd still show up. And my showing up delighted His heart because He saw that a part of me understood that He would always be there to show up to.

When we turn our attention to Jesus, good things can still happen, even when things seem bad. And when we turn our eyes upon Jesus, our ability to live from a place of contentment increases.

As I continue to develop a heart of consistent contentment, I aim to ensure that my daily life is guided by a deep sense of gratitude and trust in God's plan. It's about starting each day with a heart full of thankfulness and recognizing the blessings surrounding me, whether big or small.

Prayer is the cornerstone of my daily routine. Through prayer, I connect with God, seeking His guidance, strength, and wisdom to navigate the challenges of life. In moments of quiet reflection, I find solace in His presence, knowing He is always by my side, ready to comfort and guide me through whatever lies ahead.

At the heart of living in contentment is a deep trust in God's provision and sovereignty. It's about surrendering my desires and plans to His will, trusting He knows what's best for me, even when the path ahead seems unclear. In moments of uncertainty, I find peace in knowing God is in control, and He works all things together for my good.

Ultimately, living in contentment is a daily journey—a journey of faith, hope, and trust in God's unfailing love. It's about finding joy and fulfillment in the simple moments of life, knowing that true contentment is found in Him alone.

In Philippians 4:11-13 (NIV), Paul is in prison awaiting execution for false charges laid against him. The passage you are about to read is his thank you note to a gift he had received from the Philippian church (a community he had founded) and some awesome insight on the mystery of contentment:

"I am not saying this because I am in need, for I have learned to be content whatever the circumstances. I know what it is to be in need, and I know what it is to have plenty. I have learned the secret of be-

ing content in any and every situation, whether well-fed or hungry, whether living in plenty or in want. I can do all things through Him who gives me strength."

A great truth can be taken away from what Paul says in this scripture: Faith and contentment go hand-in-hand. A certain level of contentment must accompany your faith, especially when your faith doesn't come in the package you had expected.

When we learn to live from a place of contentment, we can live life with ease. We can live with the understanding that the God of the universe, who knows the number of hairs on our heads, knows exactly what He's doing in and through our lives. We can have faith in His plan, much like Paul did while in captivity and like my mother did throughout her cancer journey.

HOLD ON TO FAITH

When we choose to hold onto our faith and remain content, even when things don't seem to go our way, we allow that same faith to grow. How? Because of the simple fact that no matter what, we still hold on!

In the midst of your grief, I want to offer you practical ways to maintain your faith everyday.

Lean into Scripture: The Bible is a source of strength and comfort during challenging times. Spend time daily immersing yourself in God's Word, finding passages that speak directly to your situation. Let the promises of God's faithfulness and love wash over you, renewing your hope and bolstering your faith. When I needed encouragement from the Word of God, I turned to the Psalms. It's a great place to learn about the humanity of man and the divinity of God.

Stay Connected to Community: Surround yourself with fellow believers who can support you through prayer, encouragement, and practical help. Share your struggles with trusted friends or members of your church community, allowing them to walk alongside you in your journey. Together, you can find strength and solidarity in your shared faith. Easing into community was a challenging task to undertake while grieving. I was more comfortable secluding myself to deal with my raw emotions alone, but oh, what peace I found in the arms of faithful friends and family that God sent straight to me Himself.

Engage in Worship and Prayer: Make worship and prayer a priority in your daily life, even when it feels difficult. Set aside intentional time to praise God for who He is and to thank Him for His faithfulness. Pour out your heart in prayer, laying your burdens at His feet and trusting Him to carry you through. In moments of frustration, while grieving, my questions to God turned into tears, softening my heart and leading me to find unexpected blessings. As I poured out my frustrations, I began to notice the tender mercies surrounding me—the warmth of the sun and the kindness of a friend. Gradually, gratitude replaced frustration, and I was overwhelmed with thankfulness for God's presence and provision amidst my challenges.

Practice Gratitude: In the midst of hardship, cultivating an attitude of gratitude can help shift your perspective and focus your attention on God's goodness. Take time each day to count your blessings, no matter how small they may seem. Acknowledge God's faithfulness in the past and trust Him to continue working in your life. Getting a gratitude journal helped me do this consistently while subconsciously creating a list of prayer points.

Hold onto Hope: Above all, cling to the hope that is found in Jesus Christ. Remember that He is the anchor for your soul, steadfast and secure. Even in the darkest moments, trust that God is at work, weaving beauty from the brokenness and bringing light into the darkness. Keep your eyes fixed on the hope of eternity, knowing that one day, all pain and suffering will be redeemed.

I pray that these tips will help strengthen your faith and sustain you through your grief. Remember, you are never alone, and God is with you every step of the way.

A TIME TO REFLECT

1. What areas in your life are requiring you to hold out on faith right now?

   _____

   _____

   _____

   _____

   _____

2. Choose one practical way to hold onto faith above and ask God to show you how to act it out. Write out your prayer.

   _____

   _____

   _____

   _____

   _____

Confidence in the Lord—*"If our God will not deliver us..."*

7

P eople often say that your mid-20s and early 30s are the most stressful years of life. It's a critical time when individuals are settling into their careers, living conditions, and relationships. I can definitely recall and attest to the weight of most of these responsibilities at this life stage. All of a sudden, your name is the hot topic in the mailbox; you know what I mean—bills, bills, and more bills.

In a time when such responsibility is demanded of me, I often find myself reminiscing on the simpler years when my greatest responsibilities consisted of waking up on time to get to school before the morning bell, bringing an empty lunchbox home, and, most importantly, keeping my friends' secrets.

I remember my elementary school days as if it were yesterday. One day during recess, my good friend in kindergarten pulled me aside from the school park's jungle gym to have a confidential chat. You knew it was serious when a friend pulled you away from the most exciting thing on the school grounds.

With her big blue eyes piercing my soul, she said four words that would haunt my life from that moment to the rest of my earthly days: "You can't tell anyone." She told me what I believed to be her deepest, darkest secret at the time. I'll never forget how I felt or what I thought that day.

Wow. *Out of all the people in the playground, she trusted me. This is huge. Surely, I'll treasure this secret forever.*

I'd never felt a responsibility so strong until that moment. And it felt good.

I kept that secret so well. It was stored ever-so deep in the crevices of my brain, to the point that I completely forgot what the secret was, even to this day.

That's right. I'm legendary.

Although I'm sure the level of intensity of this elementary school-kept secret didn't run deep enough to change the entire course of my friend's life, there's a lot to be said about her willingness to trust me with a piece of information that was so sacred to her. She believed in my ability to keep her secret. She *chose* to trust me. I think that's huge.

Although this moment in my life seems trivial, it's an example of how we should see ourselves trusting in God. No, He isn't just a friend in elementary school. He's much more than that. He's "a friend that sticks closer than a brother" (Proverbs 18:24).

It doesn't stop there. While He calls us friends, He is also a Father, Counselor, Teacher, Provider, Waymaker, Peacemaker, and Promise Keeper. The list eternally goes on. Because this great God is all of this and so much more, we have a reason to rest confidently in Him as it concerns our lives.

REMAINING CONFIDENT AMIDST THE UNCERTAIN

Earlier on, we talked about choosing to live from a place of contentment.

Proverbs 19:21 says, *"Many are the plans in the mind of a man, but it is the purpose of the Lord that will stand"* (ESV). Understanding that our personal plans are subject to a greater plan is essential. And sometimes, the route to the greater plan is turbulent—spinning us uncontrollably, knocking our head a few times, and shocking us to our core.

Yes, you might face opposition, challenges, and trials. But this is all meant to build your faith and your inner spirit man. It's all meant to point you back to full dependency on the Source.

Living from a place of contentment has stages. I've narrowed it down to four:

RECEIVE, REMAIN, RELEASE, AND REPEAT.

Receive

You're presented with a fact, truth, or circumstance. Receiving is the choice to accept that which is presented before you, just as it is. To receive does not mean to settle and to give up. To receive is to accept. It's saying yes to embarking on an experience with what you have been presented with. To receive is a choice.

"Come now, you who say, 'Today or tomorrow we will go to such and such a city, spend a year there, buy and sell, and make a profit;' whereas you do not know what will happen tomorrow. For what is your life? Is it even a vapour that appears for a little time and then vanishes away" (James 4:13-14, NKJV).

"Do not boast about tomorrow, for you do not know what a day may bring" (Proverbs 27:1).

We are called to live for the now, so instead of solely dwelling on how a fact, truth, or circumstance might take effect in the long haul, choose to dwell on the idea that what is presented to you is simply a new experience—even if uncomfortable or unpreferred.

Sometimes, those are the best moments to open up to a new experience: when you don't really know what's on the other side of it all. Your only requirement is to live.

Live with expectation and believe that God, the Potter, controls everything. He has the power to shape your life, not only in the way that He sees fit, but also in a way that He knows suits you best. In a way that deems you fit for His use:

"But now, O Lord, you are our Father; we are the clay, and you are our potter..." (Isaiah 64:8, NKJV).

Remain

It takes a lot of strength to remain. This stage of contentment is critical; it's where you decide how to address that which has been presented to you and received by you. It is the stage where your "anchor" will be tested. This includes your values, morals, and character.

Luke 12 wonderfully illustrates the Remain stage. Before addressing a crowd of thousands of people, Jesus turns to His disciples and delivers a quick lesson, warning them about hypocrisy. Check out verses 11 and 12:

"And when you are brought to trial in the synagogues and before rulers and authorities, don't worry about how to defend yourself or what to say, for the Holy Spirit will teach you at that time what needs to be said" (NLT).

Remaining is understanding that there is a time, purpose, and place for everything. Heeding to the leadership of the Holy Spirit can help us discern timing.

Release

It takes a lot of faith and courage to release. This stage of contentment requires action. Sometimes, what the Holy Spirit says to us seems contrary to what our minds are telling us. That's because the human mind cannot comprehend a supernatural God.

To release is to let go. Release with faith and expectation, no doubt. We often categorize releasing a thing as losing or giving up, as if it comes with an automatic deficit. But it doesn't have to be this way. Choosing to release can be a confident step towards freedom. When we freely release our circumstances to God, we are proving our faith and belief in His ability to make things happen for our good. We are showing Him that we accept His will as greater than our own will and that we trust Him.

Yes, choosing to release can be tough at times, but just know that in the process, you are making room for more of what's truly yours.

Repeat

The Repeat stage is all about retracing the first three stages.

Living from a place of contentment does not mean that you are settling. Living from a place of contentment is receiving the ultimate privilege of peace. A peace in knowing that your path is already paved. A peace in knowing that your steps are already ordered. A peace that confirms your victory through Christ.

When we choose to Receive, Remain, Release, and Repeat as circumstances come and go in our lives, we learn to grow and remain confident in God and His ultimate plan for us.

"I remain confident of this: I will see the goodness of the LORD in the land of the living." (Psalm 27:13, NIV)

I believe my mother exemplified the four stages of contentment while coping with cancer. In the recording of her first-class journey, she confidently spoke about her faith in God's ability to heal her while also acknowledging her submission to His ultimate plan for her life, however, it unfolded:

"...I leave myself in the hands of God. I know God is a healer, I have no doubts, but like the three Hebrew boys said, 'If our God will not deliver us, we will not bow.' It's the same thing. I know God is a healer, but if He chooses not to, then it's something I have to accept, and maybe He's trying to show me that it's not such a bad thing."

Her words bring to mind a significant Bible story that beautifully illustrates the contentment stages we've been discussing. Daniel 3 tells the story of a powerful King Nebuchadnezzar, who makes a massive golden image in the city of Babylon. He gathers princes, governors, captains, judges, treasurers, counsellors, sheriffs, and rulers of that province to dedicate this image. From this point on, everyone in the city of Babylon was ordered to bow down and worship this image whenever they heard the sound of a cornet, flute, harp, sackbut, and the list of instruments goes on and on. Whoever disobeyed this command would be thrown into a burning fiery furnace. Three Hebrew boys, Shadrach, Meshach, and Abednego, were those daring men. They played with fire—pun intended—by refusing to bow down and worship the golden image. They were committed to only serving their God. *Our God.* For this, they were brought before a furious King Nebuchadnezzar. The king sternly reminded the three Hebrew boys that if they disobeyed his orders, they would be thrown into the fiery furnace.

Brace yourself. This is how the boys respond to the king:

"O Nebuchadnezzar, we do not need to defend ourselves before you. If we are thrown into the blazing furnace, the God whom we serve is able to save us. He will rescue us from your power, Your Majesty. But even if he doesn't, we want to make it clear to you, Your Majesty, that we will never serve your gods or worship the gold statue you have set up." (Daniel 3:16-18, NLT)

With utmost fury, the king commands that the furnace be heated up seven times hotter than usual. He then commands his strongest men to seize Shadrach, Meshach, and Abednego, tie them up, and throw them into the fiery furnace. The fire is so hot that the strong men, who threw the Hebrew boys in, die from its impact. While the three Hebrew boys are still in the middle of the fire, the king is shocked to notice four figures, unbound in the middle of the fire, when, in fact, he had ordered three bound men be thrown into the fire. *Where did the fourth person come from?* With his own mouth, the king says that the fourth figure in the fire resembles a god! So, King Nebuchadnezzar orders the boys to come out of the fire, saying, "Shadrach, Meshach, and Abednego, servants of the Most High God, come out!"

Isn't it interesting how the king of Babylon, the golden figure advocate, declared with his own mouth the existence of the Most High God? Isn't it interesting that the king recognized that these Hebrew boys were servants of this God as a result of their supernatural experience in the fire? The Hebrew boys came out of the fire spotless and unbothered, as if they'd never been thrown into such a horrific predicament.

"Then Nebuchadnezzar said, 'Praise to the God of Shadrach, Meshach, and Abednego! He sent his angel to rescue his servants who trusted in him. They defied the king's command and were willing to die rather than serve or worship any god except their own God. Therefore, I make this decree: If any people, whatever their race or nation or language, speak a word against the God of Shadrach, Meshach, and Abednego, they will be torn limb from limb, and their houses will be turned into heaps of rubble. There is no other god who can rescue like this!' Then the king promoted Shadrach, Meshach, and Abednego to even higher positions in the province of Babylon." (Daniel 3:28-30, NLT)

Wow. The three Hebrew boys were so content in God that they didn't let any person in higher authority on earth defile their reverence for and relationship with Him. In the end, the king respected the unwavering faith of these boys and, more so, the favour that was attached to their faithfulness. May our faith break barriers and open our eyes to the goodness of God.

Receive

The three Hebrew boys from the city of Babylon received the order from the king to worship the golden image when summoned. As people from this city, they knew it was a requirement, and they took this information for what it was.

Remain

BUT. The three Hebrew boys decided to remain planted in their covenant with God, refusing to worship the golden image or serve any other god. Even though opposing King Nebuchadnezzar's powerful rulership could cost them their lives, they stayed true to their values, morals, character, and God. They publicly declared their faithfulness to their one true Father, and nothing could change their minds.

Release

The three Hebrew boys did not pick a fight with the king or try to challenge the strong men who were ordered to throw them into the fire. Instead, they released their current circumstance to God, saying, "If we are thrown into the blazing furnace, the God whom we serve is able to save us. He will rescue us from your power, Your Majesty (Daniel 3:17, NLT)." And even more beautifully they added, "But even if he doesn't, we want to make it clear to you, Your Majesty, that we will never serve your gods or worship the gold statue you have set up (Daniel 3:18, NLT)." These boys knew that they served an all-seeing, all-knowing, all-powerful God, a present help in the time of trouble (Psalm 46:1). They released their circumstance into the hands of a majestic God and believed He would move on their behalf, and He did.

Repeat

As small, simple, and insignificant as this stage may seem, it's my favourite to share. The faith of the three Hebrew boys was confirmed, strengthened, and accepted after God had shown everyone that He was a boss by saving the boys from the fiery furnace. But the story doesn't end there! The level of faith that these boys exuded throughout their journey became contagious. People who witnessed the miraculous happenings, even the king, were completely amazed. I can see them now with their jaws hanging to the ground. I'm sure at this point, they were curious to know what they could do to have a relationship with this miracle-working God. The faith of the three Hebrew boys was tried, tested, and true, and as a result, the gospel spread throughout the region. More souls accepted God—our God! Talk about being fruitful and multiplying disciples.

Now, with this newfound faith, believers can walk through any situation knowing that they are never alone, and have the help of Almighty God. They can now receive, remain, and release with hope. And this hope, which will also be tried, tested, and proved to be true, can produce a new harvest of believers. That's the power of Repeat.

The four stages of contentment were also displayed throughout the course of my mother's cancer journey. Let's break this down, one more time.

Receive

After feeling abnormal for a period of time, my mother had taken several tests and evaluations, which eventually revealed that she had been experiencing the symptoms of stage-four lung cancer. As terrifying and difficult as this information may have been to process, she had to make the choice to accept the experience that came along with this reality: that cancer was now something that was a part of her life.

My mother understood that there was a new level to life that she had to master. A level that couldn't have been defeated without this new challenge before her. What was this new level? It was holding fast to the goodness of God, not only in the ideal but in the difficult. My mother had to live with the dichotomy of wanting to be well, knowing that God *could* do anything for her, and understanding that only God knew what the final outcome would be. She had to understand that at the end of the day, He could do whatever He wanted.

And whatever He chose to do would still be good. My mother had to live in the present day and trust that her Heavenly Father would take care of the rest.

Remain

My mother wasn't hasty in making decisions to solve her problem on her own. Instead, she waited on the leading of the Holy Spirit to give her instruction.

After seeking the Lord in her quiet time, she would confidently share the next steps to putting her faith into action, be it hiring a naturopath to help assist her on her desired journey to healing or buying a portable sauna to benefit from its healing properties. Mom did everything, to the best of her ability, through the lens of prayer.

Release

"I leave myself in the hands of God."

When my mother said this in the recording of her first-class journey, I believe she freed herself psychologically, mentally, physically, and emotionally from the reality of her illness. She released her cancer battle completely to God.

Repeat

With every new level of pain that befell my mother over the course of her journey, she lived out her strong faith in God. She vowed to love God past the pain, past the bad reports, and past constant opposition, and this reminded those who knew her—including me—that God could never fail His people. It is through the example of her journey that we can all find ways to endure our own hardships by applying the stages of contentment—with hope.

It takes a lot of guts to be *Godfident*—meaning, your confidence comes from God's history and abilities. You'll notice a shift in your perspective when faced with earthly challenges. Your level of joy might astound you. It will be evident at all times—unspeakable even. And it is impossible for your joy to ever be taken away.

God doesn't tell us exactly when or why we go through certain things. Instead, He launches us out into the deep waters—but He never forgets to put on our life jacket.

I've finally come to a point where I can awkwardly delight in the frightening realities of life because they are an indication of God's trust in me. He trusts me enough to place me in positions where I can demonstrate all that He has taught me up to that point. He trusts me enough to say yes to swimming in deep, stormy waters. He trusts me enough to say yes to walking through a flaming fire.

Why?

Because He sees and knows that contentment and faith, combined, is my anchor. When He sees this, it gives Him room to do supernatural things in my life.

He'll do that for you, too.

A TIME TO REFLECT

1. Read Philippians 4:11-13. Journal any thoughts that come to mind when reading this Scripture.

   _____

   _____

   _____

   _____

2. What is one thing the story of the three Hebrew boys has taught you?

   _____

   _____

   _____

   _____

3. What is one thing you need to release right now?

   _____

   _____

   _____

   _____

A Heart of Gratitude: Enjoying Sweet Journeys

8

F inding moments to be grateful along life's journey is essential to truly savour the sweetness of life, especially after a loss, when life gets hard, and it feels like nothing sweet is left.

Thankfulness.

Appreciation.

Gratefulness.

These are all synonyms of gratitude. During my grief journey, I've learned that being grateful, thankful, and appreciative is a state of being that I have to choose and commit to pursuing *daily*.

After losing our loved ones, it's easy to get caught up in the challenges of life that come with loss or the domino effect of obstacles that chase us down (and that we so desperately try to overcome). It is a constant fight to pause, reflect, and acknowledge the blessings we still have in front of us. But my friend, when you can finally do that, you'll be surprised at the profound sense of fulfillment and contentment this type of breakthrough can bring you.

Gratitude can remarkably shift our perspectives, allowing us to focus on the abundance in our lives rather than dwelling on what we feel we may lack. It invites us to appreciate the simple pleasures, the kindness of others, and the beauty surrounding us daily.

Whether it's the sun's warmth on our skin, the laughter of loved ones, or the kindness of a stranger, there are countless opportunities to be grateful.

As a believer, the gift of gratitude has personally taught me the importance of appreciating not only the moments and people in my life but also the God who grants them to me.

It has humbled me, reminding me that the very life I live is not my own.

I didn't make it.

I couldn't earn it.

I don't deserve it.

It wasn't self-produced. It reminds me that a powerful grace from God himself constantly hovers over my life. How could I not be grateful for that?

How could *we* not be grateful for that?

Believe it or not, I'm grateful to have seen my mother walk through her cancer journey, as difficult as it was. I've seen how her battle with cancer has influenced my journey with grief, and gratitude had a huge part to play in this.

Mom had her good days when things seemed normal. She also had her bad days, especially following radiation treatments, when she was overtaken by its effects and the wind was knocked out of her—so much so that she couldn't do simple things, like walk up the stairs in our home. It was quite painful to witness.

But it was just as sweet, if not sweeter, to also witness her whisper, "Thank you Jesus" when she made it to the top of the staircase, or smile at me with hope-filled eyes mid-conversation, or remind me of scripture she read earlier that day when she sensed I was losing hope. If I hadn't witnessed these subtle displays of gratitude, contrasted with the reality of her illness, I don't believe I would have been able to manage my grief journey in the way that I have.

Whether it was conscious or subconscious, on my worst days, I would remember her sweet whisper, *thank you, Jesus,* her hopeful smile, or those Bible verses she'd reminded me of in the past. My mother taught me that trusting in Jesus was beneficial in *every* season, but it required actionable gratitude.

I grew a grateful heart when I finally understood who I had in Jesus. I've learned that gratitude is inherently more than just a thought, feeling, or emotion. It involves acknowledging and appreciating something, someone, outside of ourselves—Jesus. He is the One who gives me life.

He is the One who created this life I'm living.

He is the One who sacrificed Himself and took the penalty of sin for me so that I didn't have to. And for that, I am compelled to express my gratitude.

How?

Through words. Prayer and thanksgiving. Thanking God for His loving nature, which sees me through each day, and for granting me countless blessings, whether or not I see them amidst my trials.

Through good deeds and gestures. By living a disciplined life dedicated to displaying how grateful I am for Jesus' love and sacrifice for me and staying committed to spreading this good news to the world around me so that others would come to know this great love too. My mother did a great job at that, and I sense a responsibility to carry the torch she's passed on to me.

***

As I've continued to surrender my grief journey to Jesus, He's had a funny way of chipping away at my faults. He has humbled me in ways I wasn't ready for and resurfaced some not-so-pleasant moments of mine pre-loss, for which I wasn't so grateful.

Moments I kind of regret.

I can recall the many Saturdays I'd practically been forced to go shopping with my mother—also known as the last child syndrome, when your siblings are grown and too cool to shop with their parents and also too cool to have their youngest sibling tag along with them. So I had to go. Off I went with my mother bear. With a sour attitude.

One time, after hours of shopping, my mother thought it would be cute to go to one of my favourite clothing stores. We were on a quest to find her the best-fitting skinny jeans.

We picked up almost every pair of jeans in the store. I already knew in my heart that there was no way she would walk out with a pair of skinny jeans she liked. There was no way. It wasn't her thing. She was a wide-leg or bell-bottom kind of woman. Skinny jeans just weren't her thing. She tried one pair, couldn't stand their look, and sent me back to the floor for multiple different sizes and styles. There came a point where I just couldn't take it anymore.

"I want to go home now!" I yelled.

Needless to say, that was a bratty move. Mama wasn't having that. As you can imagine, she gave me a reason to feel even more miserable leaving the mall that day.

Life as I know it has completely transformed since then.

While walking through my grief journey, it was regret from an experience like this one that eventually led me back to pursuing a heart of gratitude in *all things*.

Now, I would do anything to get that horrific day back. I would do anything for a day of shopping for skinny jeans that I knew my mother wouldn't really buy. With a renewed perspective, I'd say this "horrific" day would have been a wonderful one to relive.

I often ponder how I could have acted differently and made the best of alone time with my mother. If I had it my way now, there would be a lot more laughing and smiling and a lot less yelling and complaining.

Learn from this experience of mine, my friend. Simple moments like these leave lasting imprints on our souls. Be intentional *now* with the people in your life and the time you spend with them, no matter what you're doing. Don't take their presence for granted, even when you aren't quite enjoying yourself and you "want to go home" (whatever that means for you). Each day you have with them is an added blessing, even on the annoying and irritating days.

Living with a heart of gratitude keeps your countenance afloat. You're bulletproof. You're the oil; life's circumstances and uncertainties are the water. They just don't mix.

When we choose to be grateful, we can identify the greater purpose and the greater good in everything we encounter.

> LIVING WITH A HEART OF GRATITUDE KEEPS YOUR COUNTENANCE AFLOAT. YOU'RE BULLETPROOF. YOU'RE THE OIL; LIFE'S CIRCUMSTANCES AND UNCERTAINTIES ARE THE WATER. THEY JUST DON'T MIX.

***

One of the most captivating takeaways from the recording of my mother's first-class journey was when she explained what the presence of God felt like. She said that as she felt her body ascending, her soul began to sing:

Sweet Jesus, sweet Jesus,
What a wonder you are,

You are brighter than the morning star.

The beauty in this part of her experience is her choice of words. In a moment when others would be fearful, she chose gratitude and peace. She didn't know where she was going or what exactly was happening, but her faith told her that what she was experiencing was the Lord's doing.

Her faith told her that God was near. She was grateful for God's presence, and she acted on this gratitude by worshiping Jesus. If only we could respond to the unknowns of life in this way.

If only we could take a moment to find stability in the ruckus and refocus on what and who is sure.

If only our first response could be worship and not worry.

If only our resolve could be to fully trust the One we choose to worship.

If only our single option could be to trust Jesus—with *everything.*

Only then could we truly see the gift in gratitude, sacrifice, and surrendering our hope and expectations to God's knowledge, protection, and care. The beauty and heart of Jesus is that He is always a step ahead of us. He anticipates every step we take because He's already laid the path before us. His hope is that we would choose to follow Him *all* of our days, as good or bad as they seem. His promise is that He'll hold our hand the entire journey so we don't get lost, slip, or fall. This loving Jesus promises to be with us until the end of the world, just as He promised His disciples:

"...and lo, I am with you always, even unto the end of the world." (Matthew 28:20, NKJV)

With that, I feel strongly compelled to remind you not to wait on the "end of the world" to enjoy sweet journeys with Jesus.

His will is to journey with you *now.* Walking in step with God in a relationship and living a life that honours Him and expresses utmost gratitude daily should be our focus *now*.

When we understand God's love and how His presence can enrich our lives, we are more drawn to Him. Just like a best friend's tendencies may rub off on you after years of a fruitful relationship, Christ's character will do the same to us as we journey with Him. Having the character of Christ and having a relationship with Christ are two important factors that I believe contribute to acquiring the gift of eternal heavenly habitation.

I eagerly await going to this glorious place of eternal joy, where heavenly treasures are stored up for me and everyone who believes. What a sweet journey that will be.

Sweet Jesus, sweet Jesus, what a wonder you are.

"Fear not, little flock; for it is your Father's good pleasure to give you the kingdom." (Luke 12:32, KJV)

A TIME TO REFLECT

1. What are three things that you are grateful for today? Journal them.

   _____

   _____

   _____

   _____

2. How will you remind yourself to live in the moment as often as you can?

   _____

   _____

   _____

   _____

It's Just Pure Niceness After This

9

Does anything scare you?

I have to admit that after losing my mother, the thought of dying comes to mind a lot more often. And it kinda scares me.

Doesn't death scare everyone? Maybe not.

But I find myself asking more questions about death every now and then. Questions like...

How will I die?

Where will I be when I die?

What's going to happen to me?

When will this be?

Will I see it coming, or will it happen unexpectedly?

Another thing, a little less intense that I can't stand is spiders. Their long, creepy-crawly legs freak me out to the core. If I'm in a room in my home where they are unreachable and no one is around to help me get rid of them, I immediately exit the premises. One time, I evacuated my room for an entire week. It sounds crazy, I know, but trust me, after seeing the size of that thing, you would, too.

The thought of speaking before many people also sends me into a slight panic. This fear is real for millions around the world. Studies have shown that people fear public speaking more than they fear death. They would rather die—DIE—than speak publicly. As one who's experienced a few awkward and embarrassing public moments in my lifetime thus far, I understand how traumatic public speaking can be. I understand what transpires on the inside.

Your mind is racing. You stutter every other word. You shake uncontrollably. The list goes on.

I've realized that my fears of death, spiders, and public speaking all have something in common: in their own way, they all cause me to freeze or run away.

When wrestling with the thought of death, I become worrisome to the point that I'm unable to enjoy life to the fullest in a given moment. When spotting spiders in my personal space, I shrivel up and find the nearest exit. When presented with the opportunity to speak publicly, I doubt, deny, and duck.

Fear is a paralyzer. If given room to fester, it has the power to suck the very life out of you—like a leech that's extremely hard to detach from.

Do you want to know something else? Fear that paralyzes is nothing but a big, fat, juicy lie from the enemy. Satan. The father of lies. He works 24/7 to steal, kill, destroy, and dismantle us and everything God wants for us.

But God wants us to know that He has not given us this spirit of fear—yes, it's a spirit. This truth is shared through Apostle Paul as he encourages Apostle Timothy to continue teaching the gospel of Jesus boldly. But I think this is a truth we can all apply if we choose to live a life led by God:

"For God has not given us a spirit of fear and timidity, but of power, love, and self-discipline" (2 Timothy 1:7, NLV).

Satan wants us to accept the spirit of fear so that we operate from a place of hate rather than love. He wants us to accept the spirit of fear so that we forget that God has given us dominion over all things (including spiders). He wants us to accept the spirit of fear so that we lose control over ourselves and our minds.

But we have the right *not* to accept this spirit.

Yes, fear exists, and everyone will encounter it at some point, but we choose whether to let it shape our lives or paralyze us.

Hearing my mother address the topic of fear, particularly relating to death, had a great effect on my understanding of it. Here's a reminder of what she said:

"There is *no fear*. You don't need to fear."

"There's *nothing to fear* in this life."

But this final statement was a real head-turner:

"[Death is] *not a thing to fear*; it's something to embrace and welcome. It's so nice. It's like you're travelling first-class all by yourself."

In all of these statements, fear is mentioned as something that deserves zero attention; *No fear, nothing to fear, not a thing to fear.*

My mother said these words confidently while battling a terminal illness. I'd say that's pretty brave. I hope this serves as a lesson for you as much as it did for me.

The lesson is this: do your best not to claim fear as your own, and don't let fear paralyze you.

Maybe you've lost someone to cancer, and you're tempted to believe that's how you'll leave this world, too. Maybe you lost someone to a tragic and unexpected road accident, and it's paralyzed you from travelling on the road altogether. Maybe your last memory with your lost loved one was in a hospital, and you've made a vow to yourself never to step foot in a hospital again—even if your next reason for being in a hospital was for a joyous occasion, a baby's birth, for instance.

Death is a very real thing, and so is fear. As mortal and impressionable beings, it's quite normal to allow the realities of death to consume us and, as a result, experience immense degrees of fear. It's human. But I'm here to remind you that fear is not yours to keep. Not now, and not ever.

Understand that death is a part of life. Acknowledge fear if and when it passes by, but then let it pass by...and read on for more on overcoming the spiritual fight of fear—because that's what it is. It's spiritual.

OVERCOMING FEAR—THE SPIRITUAL FIGHT

Wrestling with fear in the mind is an act of spiritual warfare, and it's important we know how to combat this spiritual force.

2 Corinthians 10:4-5 (KJV) tells us how:

"For the weapons of our warfare are not carnal, but mighty through God to the pulling down of strong holds; Casting down imaginations, and every high thing that exalteth itself against the knowledge of God, and bringing into captivity every thought to the obedience of Christ."

Now, upon reading this Scripture, combatting the spirit of fear seems comprehensive enough to implement, right? Maybe for you, but for me, this passage was easier to read and harder to truly understand and implement.

Growing up, I battled with severe low self-esteem. I'll be honest to say that even in my recent adulthood, I've noticed its tendency to creep up in my life every now and again, especially when I'm called upon to do "big" things. Therapy has shed light on the fact that when these "big" things are presented to me, my initial thought is, *you couldn't have possibly meant me. I know there's someone who can do this way better than me, and I'm doing you a favour by saying no to this.*

The warfare presented in this example is that my low self-esteem left me in a perpetual state of deception about who I was and who God created me to be. Owning low self-esteem was an act of trusting in and relying upon this stronghold in my life, denying the truth of my identity.

I quickly learned that breaking through this stronghold could only occur through the power of effective and fervent prayer. There came a time when speaking to the mountains in my life with the understanding that the Holy Spirit was backing me up was the only option forward.

So I killed the lies with the Word of God concerning me. I centred my focus on the truth of my identity in Christ. I cast down the wicked imaginations that lived inside me and worked relentlessly to tear me down. I held captive every negative thought to the obedience of Christ. That's what changed the game for me, and that's what I rely upon when this stronghold dares to cross my way every now and then.

I think the same can apply when facing the stronghold of fear as it relates to death. To overcome the spiritual battle of fear, we must know our power and authority as believers—and the powers against us. Power and authority to overcome the dark forces of this world only come from God ("mighty through God"), and it is the power of God, working through Jesus Christ, that took the keys of *death, hell, and the grave* (Revelation 1:18). When we are aware that this power works within us (since we are made in God's likeness [Genesis 1:26]) we have the authority to cast down all imaginations that oppose God's kingdom, will, and intent for mankind. We have the authority to bring unrighteous thoughts and forces into captivity.

THE GOAL ISN'T HEAVEN; A RELATIONSHIP IS

I find it interesting that society believes that we will all make it to heaven one day. As the world grapples with the complexity of loss, one particular phrase often offered as solace stands out to me as problematic: *They're in a better place now, looking down on you.*

While intended to provide comfort, I find myself unable to subscribe to this sentiment. I've heard this phrase time and time again, used to comfort individuals who have experienced the loss of a loved one. It's been expressed to me on several occasions since my mother's passing. When I was younger, I thought it was such a beautiful way to look at death and a comforting picture to paint in my head on my worst days. But as I grew older and stronger in my relationship with Christ, that beautiful painting became blurry and dull.

***

I've never been turned away from an invite-only event before. I try to only attend events I'm positive I've been invited to. I think we should all do that.

I wonder, however, what would happen if I had the guts to sneak my way into a private event. Perhaps security would stretch their hand out and say, "Sorry ma'am, you can't enter."

Horrifying. Yet, understandable. I would have no business entering into such a place because I had no affiliation with it.

If we were to substitute heaven for this private event, I believe the same goes. I believe that heaven is a place created by God. I believe God created heaven so that He would have an environment where He could dwell with His Son, Jesus Christ, and all others who believe in His Son's name and power. But there's a requirement to dwell eternally with God.

God has to know you *want* to be there. I envision Him asking questions like:

- Did you believe that I sent my Son to die for your sins and transgressions?

- Have you been obedient to my daily instructions to the best of your abilities?

- Did you make the conscious effort to commune with me while on earth?

You must have a relationship with the Creator of heaven to go to heaven. But with all that said, the goal of life's end—or death—isn't just to go to heaven. It's to go the deepest of the deep in relationship with God, beyond the earthly realm.

Relationship. That's the point.

At the age of 17, I attended a youth retreat that changed my life. Our youth pastor preached a powerful message highlighting Matthew 7:21-23 (NKJV):

"Not everyone who says to me, 'Lord, Lord', shall enter the kingdom of heaven, but he who does the will of My Father in heaven. Many will say to Me in that day, 'Lord, Lord, have we not prophesied in Your name, and done many wonders in Your name?' And then I will declare to them, 'I never knew you; depart from Me, you who practice lawlessness!"

THE ONLY DIFFERENCE BETWEEN THOSE WHO ARE DEAD IN SPIRIT AND BODY AND THOSE WHO ARE ONLY DEAD IN SPIRIT IS THAT THE FORMER STILL HAVE A CHANCE.

The passion, truth and conviction of this message moved me to tears. It caused me to dig deep into myself.

Was I in a genuine relationship with God, or was I basing our relationship on the many things I did in His name?

By that time, I had sung on several occasions on a Sunday morning, prayed daily, and memorized some scripture, but none of that meant I earned a stamp of approval in the kingdom of heaven. Was I intentional with truly connecting with Him every day, or was I just going through the motions? Was my Monday through Saturday as "holy" as my Sunday? The answer to all of these questions was surely no. I was physically alive but spiritually dead.

That night, the Lord called me into a deeper relationship with Him. He took me in and loved me back to life. It was from this day that we built our relationship from the ground up again. And for that, I am grateful.

Several years later, I'm still walking on the relationship road. I would be lying to say that every day has been perfect ever since. But each day I wake up, I'm reminded that I have yet another chance.

Another chance to grow.

Another chance to choose to live by the spirit and not by my flesh.

Another chance to embrace a daily flourishing relationship with Christ and another chance to live the life I was called to live.

The only difference between those who are dead in spirit and body and those who are only dead in spirit is that the former still have a chance.

You're still here. That means you still have the opportunity to encounter Jesus if you haven't yet. Or re-encounter Him if you need to start fresh.

When you're spiritually alive, even death—yes, death—makes sense.

There is a Scripture that states, *"...to live is Christ and to die is gain"* (Philippians 1:21). This is spoken by the Apostle Paul as he addresses the people of Philippi in the New Testament of the Bible. He goes on in verse 22 to say, *"But if I live in the flesh, this is the fruit of my labour..."* (KJV).

To live is to know that there is always work to be done on this earth—fruitful work that is—to magnify the goodness of Jesus Christ ("to live is Christ") and increase others' joy in living for Him and serving Him. Verses 24 and 25 say: "*But to remain in the flesh is more necessary on your account. Convinced of this, I know that I will remain and continue with you all, for your progress and joy in the faith* (ESV)."

I love the posture of Paul's heart here. He's publicly declaring that he's dedicated his life's efforts to increasing people's faith in Jesus.

That is true living.

The purpose of the Christian life is to discover Christ.

To seek Him.

To find Him.

To *know* Him.

To have a relationship with Him. Most importantly, it is to share Jesus with those who do not yet know Him and to inspire those who do know Him to stay committed to the lifelong journey of knowing Him more.

When you're spiritually alive, you're aware of the fruitful labour to be done—that is, to make others aware of the gift of salvation that Jesus Christ freely gives to his children.

When you're spiritually alive, death makes sense.

To die is gain. To die is to be in eternal presence with Jesus, the One for whom we have laboured, so that others could find Him too.

To die is our reward.

Think of it like this: to die is to be reconciled with our reason for living. What a beautiful thing. Christ is more valuable than anyone or anything we will ever have in this life.

People constantly ask me how I was able to remain so strong after my mother's passing. I think it's because I was confident that my mother had a genuine relationship with Christ. I know this because her fruitful labour on this earth was evident. Her death only meant that she was granted her reward a little earlier than us.

I came across this Scripture one day, and it brought so much peace to my soul:

"Good people pass away; the godly often die before their time. But no one seems to care or wonder why. No one seems to under- stand that God is protecting them from evil to come." (Isaiah 57:1-2, NLT)

My heart breaks for those who lose loved ones and are ignorant of their eternal state. Some are fearful and tormented by the fate of their loved ones who have passed on. Some dangerously hope that heaven and hell are false truths so that they don't have to face the realities of eternity. It's a fear thing.

It is my prayer that the revelation of *God's love* finds these people.

Love, because it casts out fear, according to 1 John 4:18 (AMP):

"There is no fear in love [dread does not exist]. But perfect (complete, full-grown) love drives out fear, because fear involves [the expectation of divine] punishment, so the one who is afraid [of God's judgment] is not perfected in love [has not grown into a sufficient understanding of God's love]."

God is love. When we can embrace this truth, fear has nowhere to live in our lives.

There is **NO FEAR**. There is **NOTHING TO FEAR**. Fear is **NOT A THING**.

A TIME TO REFLECT

1. How aware are you of God's presence and power in your life right now?

    _____

    _____

    _____

    _____

2. Is there anything that you currently fear? Name it. Then, say a prayer and ask God to help you overcome it. Listen to what He says in response.

    _____

    _____

    _____

    _____

3. *"Perfect love casts out fear."* In what way does this portion of Scripture speak to you?

    _____

    _____

    _____

    _____

The Holy Spirit— He's Awesome

10

We've talked about the importance of a relationship with God, but what do we gain from this? Nothing that money can buy. Nothing that you yourself can find or conjure up.

No, instead, you get a permanent friend—a friend who sticks closer than a brother. A constant presence that alone can satisfy the unexplainable emptiness and longing in your heart. We gain the spirit of the living God.

God sent His son Jesus Christ to earth for one job: to be the ransom for our sins so that we may have eternal life. Life beyond what we know it to be here on earth as those who are subject to mortality. That is, if we choose to believe in His name (John 3:16).

Once the big job of saving humanity was finished, God wanted His son back in His rightful place—sitting at His right hand in heaven. After fulfilling His quest on earth to save the lost (that's all of us), Jesus imparted to His disciples:

"If you love me, keep my commands. And I will ask the Father, and he will give you another advocate to help you and be with you forever—the Spirit of truth. The world cannot accept him, because it neither sees him nor knows him. But you know him, for he lives with you and will be in you. I will not leave you as or- phans; I will come to you. Before long, the world will not see me anymore, but you will see me. Because I live, you also will live. On that day you will realize that I am

in my Father, and you are in me, and I am in you. Whoever has my commands and keeps them is the one who loves me. The one who loves me will be loved by my Father, and I too will love them and show myself to them." (John 14:15-21, NIV)

From the beginning of time when the earth was created in seven days, to the thousands of years leading up to the Messiah's return, to Jesus' 33 years of fruitful ministry on earth with His disciples, to the present day, there is a common theme of invitation.

God always extends an olive branch—his very own powerful arm—to invite us to live with Him. He wants to be around us but also offers us the choice to follow Him.

He extended His arm when He created our proceedors, Adam and Eve, the first humans to dwell on earth with Him to enjoy the bliss of a sinless world. Even after they fell short, He extended His arm when He sent Jesus to step in our place, undo the wreckage of sin and separation between Himself and humanity, and tear the veil. He extended His arm when he saved the Israelites on countless occasions in the Old Testament, even when they turned their back on Him and chose to serve other gods. He extended His arm when He left His promised Holy Spirit with the disciples, as seen above in John 14.

And today, He still extends His arm to anyone who believes in Him. He leaves that decision in our hands, though.

When we commit to living a life dedicated to growing our relationship with Jesus and making a conscious effort *to know Him* (Philippians 3:10-12, NLT), the quality of our lives is enriched. It's a deep thing to know God, but this can be attained in the simplest of ways. Like sitting with Him. Asking Him frequent questions. Being thankful to Him in prayer. Joining a community of believers. All of these efforts, and so many others, welcome and inflate the presence of the Holy Spirit into our lives; the Holy Spirit who Jesus, the Son of God, asked his Father, our God, to give us.

Who is the Holy Spirit?

The Holy Spirit is God's presence among His people. He gives us access to God's presence and dwells with us *through* His Spirit. The Holy Spirit is within you to teach you and guide you.

Like my mother, I believe I've been blessed with the ability and anointing to sing. All my life, I've loved to sing and have heavily believed in the power of music and worship. My siblings and I used to sing as a family group in local churches, and I've sung in choirs, praise teams, and musical plays. In all of these cases, I was singing backup or amidst a group of people. I never thought the mandate to lead a worship experience or musical would ever fall upon me. Until it did. It befell me at a time when I felt incompetent, unqualified, and unfit for the call. Yet, at the same time, I knew it was something God had already confirmed in my heart. I just felt that it was way too soon. If I've learned anything about God, it's that He runs on a completely different timeline than ours. He moves when He wants to move. So, amidst my doubt, fear, and incompetence, I had to move too.

Obeying God by *moving* has taught me to rely entirely on the Holy Spirit inside me. At times, my body trembles uncontrollably, my mind races and my heart beats way too many beats per minute. These are the opportune times to call on the Holy Spirit.

But I have to use my mouth.

The Hebrew word for spirit is *"ruah"* meaning "wind and breath." When I use my breath (spirit) to command strength from the Holy Spirit (living on the inside), my spirit is activating my Spirit.

When I'm positioned to minister, and I feel anxious, I pray a short prayer similar to this: *Holy Spirit, I know I can't do this with-*

out you. Come into my heart and do what you want to do within me. Move how you want to move. Work through me. I am an open vessel willing to be used by you.

No matter what kind of day I may have had before ministering, I always left feeling much better than when I arrived—energized, empowered, inspired, revived—like I've won a battle! I feel like I've been granted victory. That's what carrying the Holy Spirit can feel like.

THE HOLY SPIRIT IS THE COMFORTER, TEACHER, AND GUIDE

Earlier on, we read John 14:15, where Jesus tells His disciples that He would ask the Father [God] to give them an advocate to help them [and humanity] when He left Earth. In verse 26, Jesus goes on to tell the disciples how the Holy Spirit would step in for them:

"But the Comforter, which is the Holy Ghost, whom the Father will send in my name, he shall teach you all things, and bring all things to your remembrance, whatsoever I have said unto you (KJV)."

The Holy Spirit is a comforter.

You are never alone, especially when you feel an overwhelming sense of loneliness throughout your grief journey. It could be the feeling of not being fully understood by those around you or having no one around you when you feel you need them the most. Or isolating yourself from those who remain in your life to guard against any potential hurt in the future. You're not alone because the Holy Spirit lives within you. You can talk to the Holy Spirit in times of loneliness, anxiety, fear, and discouragement. 1 Thessalonians 5:17 (KJV) says, "Pray without ceasing." When you pray, you speak to the Holy Spirit while also building Him up inside of you.

Do you need comfort? Ask the Holy Spirit.

Need encouragement? Ask the Holy Spirit.

Feeling anxious? Speak to the Holy Spirit.

What I've found is that when you are willing to invite the Holy Spirit in, He always—and I mean always—shows up in unexpected ways. And it's so beautiful and thrilling. Like an unexpected gift. I recall a moment I had at the altar at my church not too long after losing my mother. I had finally gotten to the point where the reality of my new normal had sunk in, and the energy I had left was only enough to ask God for strength and peace for the daunting journey ahead. I remember rushing to the altar calmly in appearance but desperately in heart. I remember placing my hands on the altar, closing my eyes, and praying one of hundreds of my honest prayers to the Lord.

Then, something happened. I felt a hand rest on my right shoulder.

Your first thought is likely, *oh that's nice, someone came to pray for her.* That would be an everyday thing at my church, which is why I thought that too—until I cracked the corner of my eye to peep at what was behind me in my peripheral. To my shock, no one was there.

Absolutely no one.

Tears immediately burst down my face like shooting stars. I immediately knew it was the Lord's soft and gentle touch reassuring me of His presence. I imagined Him saying, "There, there, my child. I hear you, and I'm here for you—right now and always."

I needed nothing more than to know that He was with me and that He could hear me as I practically begged for His help to guide me through such a challenging time. And in that moment, He proved Himself to be both present and my comforting and loyal Father. I encourage you to leave room for Him to prove this to you, too.

The Holy Spirit is a teacher.

What's the first picture that comes to mind when you hear the word "teacher?" Perhaps it's a figure facing a blackboard with chalk or a pointer in-hand. Maybe you think of an apple on a desk. Or a keener with glasses and a stack of books under their arm. How does envisioning the aspects of a teacher relate to the Holy Spirit, you ask? Well, for one, both are deeply trusted—a teacher, by the general society and the Holy Spirit, by those who identify as believers of the Godhead.

We put our complete trust in teachers. Think about it—our parents left us in the care of these practical strangers for hours upon hours each day at the most vulnerable stages of our lives. In kindergarten, we were what? Four years old? Oh, what trust our parents displayed. But why? Why did they trust teachers so much to leave us in their care, even though they didn't fully know them?

Approval. To take it a step further, approval from the government, which funds these teachers. They gain parents' trust with statements like, "We've screened these individuals, tested their ability to teach and guide your children, and hold them accountable to our standards and expectations for public care." The parent expects that the teacher has a degree of knowledge adequate to help their child reach an expected level of success.

We trust teachers because our societal authorities trust them.

Can't we look at the Holy Spirit, our Teacher, similarly?

In our most vulnerable states, which I'd argue is every moment we as proclaimed believers live in this world of sin, we are left in the care of the Promised Holy Spirit that Jesus left with us—and left within us.

This indwelling Holy Spirit is trusted by God, our ultimate authority. This same Holy Spirit was with Jesus when He willingly gave Himself on the cross. This same Holy Spirit was with Jesus, who endured the cross.

The Holy Spirit was part of what it took for Jesus to overcome, and it is now with us to help us overcome, too—to help us get through this stage of life and the next. We trust the Holy Spirit, the Teacher, because we trust God, the Governer of our lives.

Teachers invest in our ability to apply the knowledge they give us. There is a time for teachers to inundate us with everything we need to know concerning a subject or lesson, but there's also a time for us to apply our knowledge. In those times, the teacher steps back and keeps quiet while silently prompting us to figure things out and show the work it took to get there. This lesson might be new to us, so we'll struggle every now and then, but teachers are always right there to step in when absolutely necessary—not too often, though—the reason being that they want to stretch our ability to assess and reason as we inch our way to the expected end.

Isn't that like the Holy Spirit? He empowers us with the knowledge, nature, and likeness of Christ to make decisions in our lives, yet at a point, quietly retracts the intensity of His voice to see how we will proceed. The projected and distinct voice we once heard becomes a sweet whisper or a still, small voice. He gracefully leads us along while observing our willingness to walk in step with what we already know and what we choose to hear.

Teachers never leave you the same way you were when you found them. Unless you were homeschooled, you weren't taught by the same teacher from kindergarten up to grade 12. For each new grade level, you were introduced to a new teacher, and this teacher worked with you at your current level of knowledge to start, gradually guiding you to your next level of genius.

The theme here is transformation. From grade level to grade level. Glory to glory—that's the Holy Spirit's destination—and that's the Holy Spirit's way of working in your life. He works alongside you and within you to draw out your best possible outcome. He leaves you better than you found Him. He is invested in your ability to learn, exercise, and apply wisdom. Best of all, He can be trusted.

A great way to build trust with anyone is to observe their actions, test their motives (respectfully), and recount their history. The same goes for building trust in the Holy Spirit's ability to teach and guide us. Yes, I said we need to build trust in the Holy Spirit.

I'd love to say the moment that we say yes to God is the moment we wholeheartedly trust everything He is and everything He does in our lives, but the reality is that it can become challenging to trust the Holy Spirit's ways at times—because we're not fully aware of His ways all of the time. His ways often seem more contrary to our expectations and desires, and I don't think we're always honest enough with ourselves to accept that. Thankfully, God knew us well enough to leave His Word with us.

His Word is the gift that keeps on giving. It's the one source we can trace back to know His heart's ponderings concerning the world He created. It's the tangible source He gifted us that the Holy Spirit (within us) can bear witness to.

I know you've felt that before. When you read the Bible, the words literally jump out of the page at you. You are so captivated by the life that resides in the holy scriptures that you can't help but read on. You feel a bubbling in your belly when you resonate so strongly with the text. If you haven't experienced this before, I pray you do.

The Bible is the holy book that teaches us the mystery of God. Reading it requires our full attention, which allows us to ponder and ask thought-provoking questions—especially in times when we desperately crave answers from God, like in times of grief.

Believers are commanded to meditate on the Word of God day and night (Joshua 1:8). When we meditate on the scriptures, we allow the Holy Spirit to step in as our Teacher. The Spirit helps us understand exactly what God tells us through His Word. As we dig deeper into the Word of God and allow the Holy Spirit to teach us, we grow in wisdom and strengthen our daily Christian walk.

The Holy Spirit is an accountability partner.

Before we get into the Holy Spirit's role as an accountability partner, I have a very serious question for you. Do you have an accountability partner? A person, or people, you've given the right to keep you accountable to getting things done or follow through with a commitment you've made? It's a great thing to have an accountability partner. I'd consider finding one if your answer to my question was no. And it's mainly because you'd be a maniac to think you can fully trust yourself to stay on top of everything you've committed to. Sorry—you're not a maniac. Just delusional. Sorry—not delusional. You're just a lot more optimistic than the rest of us.

Everybody needs somebody, even those we deem the most capable of taking care of us. Teachers need teachers—or need them at some point throughout their journey towards becoming teachers. Therapists need therapists. Doctors need doctors.

Imagine a doctor trying to perform heart surgery on themselves. It's just not a thing. It will never be a thing. A doctor can likely identify an area of dysfunction in their body that determines their need for heart surgery, but they would need to trust another doctor to perform tests and conclude that that's the next best step. It would be difficult to reach such a conclusion on their own. So many touchpoints are required to get an ailing person back on the road to recovery. But they couldn't do it alone.

Everybody needs somebody.

The ill doctor might need another doctor to perform surgery, but they might also need a family member to hold them account-able for staying up-to-date with their check-in appointments.

The real truth is that without accountability, we're all com-fortable with occasionally letting ourselves down.

Maybe you aren't a sick doctor in need of an accountability partner to stay on top of your appointments. Maybe your situa-tion is a little more mild. Maybe you sound a little more like this:

It's okay to skip the gym for another day.

It's okay to work on my dreams next year.

It's okay to hand that assignment in a little late.

It's okay to go back to that abusive relationship. They've changed.

It's okay to skip my Bible plan for today. God knows my heart.

Do any of these statements sound even slightly familiar?

I hate to break it to you, but these are the things that peo-ple with little to no accountability say. So again, I say, find an ac-countability partner!

There are no rules to finding the perfect accountability part-ner. They can be a friend, a family member, a work colleague, or a therapist. The main requirement here is that they are committed to your growth and ability to make progress with whatever area in life you've decided to conquer, and they're determined to see you see it through—even if that means they have to be a thorn in your side all the while.

A thorn in your side is a constant jab, like a dagger in your side that isn't going anywhere. It almost feels like it's supposed to be there since it's always been there. It's as if the thorn is there to constantly remind you of something very important. It's as if it's there to steer you in the right direction.

I'm not speaking from experience by the way. All imagination. I'm also channelling Paul, in 2 Corinthians 12:5-10, when he alludes to a thorn in his flesh as the thing that kept him from becoming self-righteous. This thorn in his flesh reminded him that he was flawed and that Jesus, the One he served with his entire life, was not (Jesus was perfect).

Paul was a wise man, and God spoke to him greatly. Of all the people in his time, he was the one who could have probably boasted about himself and not been challenged by others. But the distinguished Paul said:

"I will boast about a man like that, but I will not boast about myself, except about my weaknesses. Even if I should choose to boast, I would not be a fool, because I would be speaking the truth. But I refrain, so no one will think more of me than is warranted by what I do or say, or because of these surpassingly great revelations. Therefore, in order to keep me from becoming conceited, I was given a thorn in my flesh, a messenger of Satan, to torment me. Three times I pleaded with the Lord to take it away from me. But he said to me, 'My grace is sufficient for you, for my power is made perfect in weakness.' Therefore I will boast all the more gladly about my weaknesses, so that Christ's power may rest on me. That is why, for Christ's sake, I delight in weaknesses, in insults, in hardships, in persecutions, in difficulties. For when I am weak, then I am strong (NIV)."

The thorn in Paul's side reminded him of his weakness. He was merely a human being in need of God's grace every day. He was not Jesus, but he was who he was (as I said, a distinguished man) *because of* Jesus.

The thorn in Paul's flesh would never allow Paul to forget that very important reality and truth: Jesus was the real boss. Always has been. Always will be.

And if we know anything about a good boss, it's that they care about those they lead with such nobility. They ensure that they pass on profound lessons, skills, and practices they've learned and mastered to those after them. I'd like to believe Jesus passed on the practice of *good* accountability when He left us all, including His disciples, with His Holy Spirit. He left us with His Word. He left us with the truth. It is this Word of Truth that we can draw from to live a surrendered life. And it is the Holy Spirit who will bear witness with the Word of Truth when we read it. He helps us walk this life out. I feel so safe, so empowered in the moments I'm reminded that I'm not walking this life alone.

I have the Holy Spirit in me to comfort, protect, and guide me. I have the Word as a *lamp for my feet, a light on my path* (Psalm 119:105), and I can talk to Jesus at any time and be confident in the fact that He can hear me.

I didn't have much to say to Him in the early stages of losing my mother, but over time, the Holy Spirit did a work in my heart; making my heart of stone a heart of flesh again. I gradually got back to a place where I was able to fight past my feelings, open my mouth, and tell Him that I was simply grateful to make it another day, even when my fractured heart felt like it was failing me.

While praying those simple prayers, the Holy Spirit, my most trusted accountability partner, tenderly reminded me of Psalm 73:26, which says, *"My flesh and my heart may fail, but God is the strength of my heart and my portion forever* (NIV)."

There had been other times I'd talk to the Lord because the weight of confusion as a result of my loss was just too heavy to carry. I pleaded with Him for direction and a steady hand-hold so that I would not be led astray in life without the presence of my mother, who was such a grounding force in my life. In these moments, the Holy Spirit would remind me of Isaiah 41:10, which says, *"So do not fear, for I am with you; do not be dismayed, for I am your God. I will strengthen you and help you; I will uphold you with my righteous right hand* (NIV)."

I also felt an overwhelming sense of discouragement after losing my mother so suddenly. My zeal for life took a turn, and I became engulfed by the belief that there was no point in enjoying anything or anyone, chasing after dreams, or holding onto deep desires. To me, it seemed all for naught. It'd all die or discontinue at some point anyway. But there came moments when I began to miss that zeal for life. It was kind of a pain to live without it.

So I spoke to God about it. In these moments, the Holy Spirit would remind me of Romans 15:13, which says, *"May the God of hope fill you with all joy and peace in believing, so that by the power of the Holy Spirit you may abound in hope* (ESV)."

Do you see the theme here?

When you talk to Jesus, the Holy Spirit has a way of revealing the truth of God's Word to you and inflating your faith so that you will believe what it says.

Reading God's Word is so crucial because it enables the Holy Spirit to work in your life. As my mom says in her own book, *The Holy Spirit (in a Nutshell)—He's Awesome*:

"When you fill your heart with the Word, you'll be able to pray using the Word. The Spirit cannot operate on what is not there; He [the Spirit] needs the Word—they go together."[7]

Amazing! An inflating, strengthened spirit requires time spent in the Word and constant prayer influenced by the scriptures that the Father sent. But this doesn't just happen in a believer's life.

---

7 Dinnall, Nysley. *The Holy Spirit (In a Nut Shell): He's Awesome.* 2000.

It takes practice.

It takes dedication.

It takes dusting yourself off and going at it again and again.

I've alluded to being raised in a Christian home a few times so far. I'm extremely grateful for this today because it helped me build a desire for communion with God, no matter what life stage or experience I find myself in.

I'm grateful for family devotions on weekend mornings. I'm grateful for the round-table talks at the dinner table, which reflected God's goodness towards our family. I'm grateful for family prayer time. I'm grateful for the extended community of believers my parents kept close, who then became like family to all of us. I'm grateful for the Bible camps and retreats that took up my summer evenings.

The many years of being encouraged to fear God, develop a personal prayer life, and devote myself to reading scripture have sustained my Christian walk, especially in times of difficulty.

I'm not perfect, but I can confidently say that I've gradually learned how to let the Word of God dictate my stance while grieving, not my feelings. Yes, I had feelings, and yes, I felt pain. But that's not what I allowed to guide me for the rest of my days, post-loss—as painful as this loss was.

I had the Holy Spirit to hold me accountable and help me overcome my tendency to trust my false outlook on life after loss. Shout out to the Holy Spirit. There's nothing like Him.

A TIME TO REFLECT

1. Which characteristic of the Holy Spirit explained in this scripture resonates with you most (Comforter, Teacher, or Accountability Partner)?

   _____

   _____

   _____

   _____

2. Consider the characteristics of the Holy Spirit that you chose in the previous question. How can you ask the Holy Spirit to activate this characteristic in your life right now?

   _____

   _____

   _____

   _____

My Mother's Death Gave Me Life

11

W hen we truly perceive faith for what it is—without over-complicating it or attaching unnecessary conditions—we will grasp its true significance and power.

I enjoy travelling. I enjoy the feeling of being elsewhere, thousands of miles away, immersed in a culture and way of living that is contrary to my own.

One thing I can do without when travelling is boarding the main mode of transportation used to go the distance. You know, those giant things with wings and a tail that fly in the air for hours, even days at a time.

Airplanes.

Think about it. You're signing up to be placed in this massive thing that shoots up in the sky, and through the power of technology and smart engineering, it gracefully glides in the sky—most of the time.

The longest flight I've ever been on was 12 hours. Then, after a two-hour layover, I was up in the air for another eight hours. This was a very exciting time, as I was headed to South Africa. I'm pretty sure the days leading up to my flights to South Africa consisted of my most earnest prayers. I literally asked myself why I paid good money to basically give my life away. I know this is a horrible way to think, but I kid you not, I thought to myself: *How could you do this? You're so young and full of life. You have so much more to give.*

Travel day eventually came. With fear and trembling, I boarded the plane. The first few hours of the plane ride were a lot smoother than I presumed—that's until the plane started rocking in mid-air.

No, I thought, *it couldn't be. The flight was going so well.* It was unexpected.

What I dislike about turbulence the most isn't necessarily how it makes me feel—which is traumatizing—because it feels like the plane is bumping into rocks, whereas you're in the open sky, and there's only air and clouds. It's the fact that I can't go anywhere to escape the madness.

When turbulence occurs, passengers are commanded to return to their seats immediately and fasten their seatbelts. Great. So I'm fastening myself to die. Sorry for the morbidity; unfortunately, these were my exact thoughts at that moment. The turbulence was at an all-time high, so I had no choice but to use the only weapon I had carried with me: prayer.

I thought my most powerful prayers had been lifted to God *before* boarding the plane—but boy, was I wrong. I prayed until I had no more words. All I had left was the name of Jesus. So I used it. Again and again. I whispered His name consistently while securely buckled in my aisle seat.

I remembered how I felt while praying. I was torn. I wanted to wholeheartedly believe every word I was praying. I wanted to believe God would anoint the pilots' hands and allow each passenger to reach their destinations harm-free. Even though I did believe, there was still a part of me that wondered if God would truly save us should anything tragic happen.

What if God decides not to save us from tragedy? What if the turbulence has enough power to take us all down?

I kept praying, *God, You know my desire at this moment, but let Your ultimate will be done. I don't know what's going to happen, but I know that what ends up happening is what You allow. I will rest in You.*

It took a lot of strength (and I guess, in some ways, a lot of faith) to pray that. I couldn't even say it with my mouth. I prayed in my head. I had to keep it inside because it was too daunting to say that I was okay with dying, and it was hard to believe that would be God's will for my life.

But the peace I felt after internally confessing my acceptance of God's decision to do whatever He wanted to do with my life was unexplainable. I felt so confident, I could have taken off my seatbelt—but don't worry, I didn't. I'm happy to report that I made it through both flights in one piece and had the South African trip of a lifetime. It's still my favourite one yet.

My terrifying plane ride oddly correlates with my mother's cancer journey. Track with me.

The plane ride symbolizes her life. Like planes, life is an avenue for adventure. It can take you anywhere, and the possibilities are endless. The turbulence signifies the sickness that befell

FAITH CAN BE TOUGH. YOU DON'T EXACTLY KNOW WHERE YOU'LL LAND, BUT YOU WILL COME TO UNDERSTAND WHAT FULL DEPENDENCE ON GOD IS ALL ABOUT. IT'S A BEAUTIFUL JOURNEY.

my mother. In an instant, life was unexpectedly shaken up, and my mother had to decide how she would cope. Her response to cancer (turbulence) signifies her dependence on God. My mother activated the weapon of prayer to battle through her turbulent experience, just like I did on the airplane. The overall outcome of my crazy plane ride and my mother's cancer journey demonstrated the great impact of the powerful weapon of prayer—paired with a whole lot of faith.

Faith can be tough. You don't exactly know where you'll land, but you will come to understand what full dependence on God is all about. It's a beautiful journey.

Think of it: if everything in your life was perfect and you always knew what was going to happen next, what good would your faith be? Would you even think you'd need God? Probably not. But the way life is set up, not knowing exactly what tomorrow holds, causes us to exercise our dependence on...something.

What is that for you?

Is it yourself? Is it your spouse? Is it your job or your boss?

I hope it's God the Father. He's the all-knowing, all-seeing One who reaches down to us, waiting for us to see Him and shoot our weighty arms back up to Him.

I've come to understand that sometimes God allows situations to befall us in life just so that He can see our true response. Will we look to Him? Will we reach out to Him? Will we count it all joy (James 1:2)? Or will we count it all misery? You see my friend, troubles come, yes. But you can overcome them when you rely on the One who has overcome the world (John 16:33).

My mother's cancer journey made her more aware of God's infinite power, love, and goodness. She articulated her discovery of this while explaining her first-class trip to me. She said: *"Sometimes God puts you through some stuff to let you know that He's there."*

I see that now. I believe that now.

***

Hearing my mother's first-class trip with the Lord for the first time changed my life. I'd never heard anything like it. I felt like I was missing out on the experience of a lifetime, and I craved to feel what she felt in those moments. The only thing was that

I knew my mother was on a different dimension of spirituality than I had been. Like, ever.

I felt the need to level up.

I decided I had to find out how to mirror, or at least come close to the nature of my mother's relationship with God. I'd been talking about the importance of having God in my life, but it was time to truly *be* about it.

I felt like I was in a breeding season for new beginnings. It was time to become the best version of myself with God's help.

My mother was really good at *being* about it. She exemplified what it meant to live life by faith and commit to a growing relationship with Christ—and she made it look effortless. I remember some mornings I'd hear her singing sweet melodies to her Father throughout our home. I remember the afternoons I would hear her on the phone encouraging a brother or sister-in-Christ with the Word of God, sharpening their faith. I remember the evenings I would sneak into her room in the wee hours of the morning and find her studying scripture.

In all of my observations, one consistent thing I noticed about my mother's faith journey is the unspeakable joy that beamed out of her most days. It was evident that her faith took her to a wonderful place that couldn't be shaken or affected by a mere, earthly experience—and I needed to go to that place.

So now I'm on a faith mission. I'm committed to doing the work to enrich my spiritual journey, day by day. The beauty of venturing on such a journey is that while here on earth, there's no concrete destination. It's ongoing. Once you're in, there's no room for separation. If I fall, I can get back up again.

In Romans 8:38-39 (NLT), the Apostle Paul says:

"And I am convinced that nothing can ever separate us from God's love. Neither death nor life, neither angels nor demons, neither our fears for today nor our worries about tomorrow—not even the powers

of hell can separate us from God's love. No power in the sky above or in the earth below—indeed, nothing in all creation will ever be able to separate us from the love of God that is revealed in Christ Jesus our Lord."

We can rest completely in Jesus by and *through* faith, and as long as we do that, everything goes according to plan—according to Him.

As I've mentioned earlier on this journey of ours together, many people have asked me how I've been able to remain so strong after losing my mother to cancer. Some said they would have lost their minds had they walked in my shoes. I was extremely close to losing my mind as well. I faced thoughts of utter disbelief, denial, loneliness, and worthlessness. I questioned the reason for my existence since the person who pushed me into this world was taken away and gone forever. On the flip side, this tragic experience increased my faith levels, and they continue to evolve as the days, months, and years go by. Grieving my mother's death was an opportunity to rediscover and redefine the meaning of life. How it all began. Why we're here. What the point of each day is.

It's around Holy Week (the week leading up to Good Friday and Easter Sunday) that I'm immediately humbled when I think about the gift of life. It's around this time that I ask myself, *how often did you acknowledge Christ's sacrifice from last year's Holy Week to now?* I don't do this to condemn myself, though I may have had the tendency to at times. I do this to sharpen my focus on what my personal convictions tell me are important to observe. This is one of them.

It's never fun to conclude that I've barely acknowledged Christ's sacrifice, whether it be in my prayers or verbally sharing the gospel with those who don't yet know Jesus. No fun, because I want to believe that I've been the perfect Christian since the beginning of my walk and I've gotten everything right. But let's be real; that's just not the case for any of us.

I'm not perfect. You're not perfect. We're not perfect. And since we're human, we have the tendency to forget.

I don't mean to speak for the whole community of believers, but the truth is that only a very small fraction of us are likely to remember to thank Jesus for the sacrifice He made on the cross each and every day. If you're part of that small fraction, a huge kudos to you, and please share your daily holiness routine.

Some of us tend to forget how important this price that Jesus paid was. We forget how much Jesus went through for our sake. Yet, after losing my mother, I felt as though I had become hyper-aware of the gospel and the power of the work of the cross more than I ever had been.

I began to see the pattern of how death always leads back to life—case in point, the resurrection of Jesus three days after enduring the cross.

My mother's death reminded me of the fact that I have life in Christ. This experience reminded me that there is this life, this abundant life, that I had yet to tap into. The unfortunate reality is that it took something so painful to unravel this truth for me, but I don't think this pain was a waste. Even though there is pain and loss, there is also an opportunity to experience newfound life at the end of it all—rather, *through* it all.

Job said it best:

"...Naked I came from my mother's womb, and naked shall I return. The Lord gave, and the Lord has taken away; blessed be the name of the Lord (Job 1:21, ESV)."

The Lord does give and take away, but one thing I've noticed, both in Job's story and in my own journey of grieving my mother, is that even though He takes away, there is still something sweet in the takeaway.

Job, once the richest man on earth who had the life anyone would want, became severely ill and lost all of his possessions and his family, all because God was willing to put Job's faith to the test. But Job's "takeaway" led him to a deeper faith and later gave him double of everything that he had lost before his test.

Losing my mother was a dreadful experience, but this "take-away" guided me to my deeper faith, just like Job. If the Lord had not taken away, I don't think I'd see life the way I do now. I'm not confident I'd hold onto God with the tightest grip (even a pinky hold) in every situation, *no matter what.*

It could have only been a situation so intense and gutting as the loss of my mother that got me to this point of doing life with Jesus. To the corps. Because He proved He was willing to do life with me by hanging on the cross. Literally to the corps.

And He didn't have to, He *wanted* to.

To know He loves me that much is enough for me. That's where my peace comes from. That's where my joy comes from. That's where my hope comes from.

So, this is why I'm strong.

I'm strong because God has proven time and time again that victory lies on the other side of the test. Even in the case of death, there is yet a budding of new life.

The very words you read in this book are a testament to the manifestation of a purpose fulfilled by a fruitful and dedicated life, now at rest. My mother left this earth, but she also left her legacy—and the unexpected gift of her timely first-class trip with Jesus a month before her departure—behind. If she did not leave then, there would be no immediate urgency to share the very words on these pages.

I'm so grateful that I serve a God who finds purpose in every-thing—and I mean everything.

A TIME TO REFLECT

1. Can you remember a time when you prayed one of your most intense prayers? What were you praying about?

   _____

   _____

   _____

   _____

2. How did you feel after praying this prayer? Why do you think you felt this way? What shifted?

   _____

   _____

   _____

   _____

3. How has Jesus' sacrifice on the cross marked your life?

   _____

   _____

   _____

   _____

Airplane Runways—A Renewed Lens on Grief

12

As I continue to walk through my grief, I've noticed a transformation in how I see it. It's looking less like a stormy day and more like an airport runway.

By the way, can you tell I'm obsessed with talking about travelling and planes?

Anyway, let me explain.

Airport runways are very long and feel unending. When you think about it, it's kind of crazy how they were designed so cleverly that they can guide planes of different shapes and sizes to take off and land successfully.

Have you ever been on a plane, about to take off or land, seen all the multi-coloured lights on the ground, and wondered what they all meant? Well, today's the day you learn about what *most* of them mean. It's time for a mini crash course on runway lighting.

There are Runway End Lights, the row of lights built into the endzone of the runway that warn the pilot they are approaching the end of the runway. Runway End Identifier Lights, two flashing lights on each end of the Runway End Lights that help the pilot identify the end of the runway at a distance. Runway Edge Lights, a row of white lights along each side of the runway. Centreline Lights are white lights that run along the centreline of the runway. Touchdown Lights. Approach Lighting Systems. And so on and so forth. I won't go any further; I'm trying to land this plane—pun absolutely intended.

I know that was a lot of information, but don't worry—there isn't a pop quiz. I briefly explained the functionalities of runway lights to illustrate that each and every one of these lights offers a unique and crucial purpose: to help pilots safely take off and land airplanes—in this case, to land. We couldn't travel anywhere confidently or successfully without these lights!

I mentioned that grief is starting to look a lot less like a stormy day and a lot more like an airport runway. Throughout my grief journey, I've understood grief as my guiding light—runway light—back to God.

With every emotion felt—every feeling of pain, suffering, heartbreak, anger, fear, worry, lament, and defeat, the Lord showed me His very best quality: His nature and ability to be present with me in and through *everything*. He didn't always speak directly to me or give me all the answers I had been poking Him for, but He promised to be there, and He was.

He promised to walk alongside me to feel what I felt, and I felt Him there. He promised to comfort me in uncommon ways and through surprising and divine connections and reconnections, and I felt His presence even in that. I now have a greater understanding of the verse in Hebrews 4:15 that says: "*For we do not have a high priest who is unable to empathize with our weaknesses, but we have one who has been tempted in every way, just as we are— yet he did not sin* (NIV)."

Jesus was tempted by Satan with food, fame, and fortune immediately after getting baptized (Matthew 4). He knew what it felt like to have everything at the tip of his fingers and still turn it all away with and by the strength and Spirit of God. He conquered all of this and later left His spirit with us to walk through our own trials and temptations.

How comforting it is to know that the One who had the power to conquer all still had to live through the human experience and face a series of tests also.

The beauty of having God's presence is knowing that He will never lead us astray but always lead us to safety, just like the runway lights guide pilots for safe landings and takeoffs.

Grief led me back to Jesus, the Guiding Light of my life.

IS GRIEF SHORT, LONG, OR A LIFETIME JOURNEY?

Many people have asked me the question, "Does grief last forever?"

Strangely enough, I feel that airport runways can also bring context to help land my answer to this very difficult question. Airport runways—even the journey towards airport runways, are very long.

Picture yourself in the plane once more. You anticipate taking off, but after feeling the plane crawl ever so slowly, stop, start rolling again, and take multiple turns, you begin to get a little frustrated. You think to yourself, *how have we still not reached the runway?*

But then you do.

The engine begins to roar, and the plane feels like a rollercoaster, reaching hundreds of kilometres per hour in just seconds—yet even though you're going so fast, you feel as though this speedy blaze on the ground is longer than it should be and the pilot could be running out of runway before ascending into the open sky.

That's how grief works. Some days, it's a crawl. On other days, it's start and stop. Then we're rolling again.

Then, there are days with multiple twists and turns. And because all of these days are different, there's never really a consistent pattern that you can adjust to—which can make you feel anxious and annoyed from time to time. You think to yourself, *How am I still dealing with this? Will I ever feel better?*

But then, eventually, a day comes when you do. Your spirit man is replenished and you feel ready to take off at the speed of *life.*

Yet turbulence still comes, bringing interference to your journey of long-awaited bliss up in the clouds. It's so strong that your steady flight of renewed joy must come to a landing, and your confidence in the Pilot to land you safely starts to dwindle.

Thankfully, the Pilot does land you safely, and as a first-class complimentary gift, He offers you a care package to help you cope with the PTSD you now have to overcome on the ground as you prepare for your next flight...whenever that is. The package is filled with a travel mug and a camomile tea bag inside—peace. A plush, furry robe—comfort. And a mini Tickle Me Elmo, just for laughs—joy.

It's a few months later, and you're ready to take off again for your next destination in the land of grief. And the cycle continues.

Grief is a lifelong journey of takeoffs and landings to several different destinations. Grief revisits. It'll always try to find you. And even though you don't want to be found by it, it's your willingness to welcome it any way that makes the entire journey worthwhile—because when you say yes to this adventure, you'll find that you'll learn a whole lot about yourself, and God.

My friend, I urge you to see the journey of grief as one that does not exist to defeat you, but one that exists to guide you to your best landing. To guide you to your heart's true Home.

"The Lord is near to the brokenhearted and saves the crushed in spirit." (Psalm 34:18, ESV)

A TIME TO REFLECT

1. What picture or scenario comes to mind when you think about the ebbs and flows of grief (Ex. Airplane take-offs and landings)?

   _____

   _____

   _____

   _____

2. How do you feel about grief as something that doesn't have a definite ending?

   _____

   _____

   _____

   _____

3. What is one thing grief and loss have taught you? How has this impacted the way you live your life now?

   _____

   _____

   _____

   _____

Epilogue

Why did I title this book *The Unexpected Gift: What My Mother's Death Taught Me About Life?*

Well, I was going to call it *Riding First Class: What My Mother's Death Taught Me About Life,* but I later felt that this title didn't fully encapsulate the story behind how this book was born.

Yes, my mother shared her first-class journey with me, and it impacted how I see and live life now, but there was more to the story that I needed you, my friend and reader, to know.

I needed you to know that throughout this entire experience and journey, from my mother's lung cancer diagnosis to this present day (and those to come), I have experienced many unexpected things. Things I thought would destroy me—yet somehow built me up for the better. All of these occurrences, packaged and wrapped in one, made for the perfect gift of renewed perspective and purpose.

Let's walk through this unexpected series of events one last time, shall we?

My mother's death—unexpected. My mother's first-class trip with Jesus—unexpected. The blessing of capturing an audio recording of my mother's first-class trip a month before her passing—unexpected. The recording of my mother's first-class trip becoming a steady source of healing throughout my grief journey—extremely unexpected. All of this is to say that the best gifts are unexpected ones. The ones you don't see coming.

My greatest disappointment in life has taught me my greatest life lesson.

My mother's death highlighted [with the brightest-coloured neon highlighter] the necessity of having a steady and consistent relationship with God. When we have a genuine relationship with our Father, we do not need anything this temporal world has to offer, and disappointing life experiences do not everlastingly destroy us.

I want you to know, whether you've lost someone or you battle with fearing for your own life, that death of any form is not the end if you have a relationship with Jesus. In fact, it's just the beginning of your eternity.

I want to ignite a fire in your spiritual journey, and if you're already on it, I want to add thick logs to your pit.

Be encouraged to live your life out loud, with full confidence in the God who placed you here to live it! Enjoy sweet journeys with the ones you love. Be content in every season that you face. Choose to live with the awareness of God's fullness and what His presence in your life brings.

There is so much more to live for. So much more than you think.

Enjoy your journey, and may it pave the path to a fruitful and eternal legacy.

I F YOU'RE READING THIS, WE'VE GOT A BONUS FOR YOU!

Near to the end of her journey, my mother took a first-class trip with Jesus. To honour her story, I've published the audio recording for your reading experience. You can listen by visiting the URL below, which will take you to the audio recording. Whether you're grieving, reflecting, or simply seeking comfort, I hope this recording offers you peace, perspective, and a reminder that God's presence never leaves us.

Listen to the full audio recording at:

thelifejournal.ca/book-exclusive

About Caroline

Caroline is a writer, creative, and host of the Care to Talk podcast. Through her blog, The Life Journal, and her storytelling, she explores faith, grief, and personal growth. *The Unexpected Gift: What My Mother's Death Taught Me About Life* is her debut book, a heartfelt reflection on the lessons she learned after the sudden loss of her mother due to a cancer battle. Caroline is passionate about helping others navigate life's challenges through faith, grace, and wisdom.

When she's not writing or deep in conversation about life's big questions, you can find Caroline wandering new places with a fork in hand, savoring flavors from around the world. A true artist at heart, she loves bringing ideas to life—whether through crafting, painting, or any creative project that lets her hands do the storytelling.

Caroline's Personal Note to Readers

Thank you for reading The Unexpected Gift. My hope is that it encouraged you to embrace the beauty in life's hardest moments. I'd love to hear your thoughts—feel free to connect with me!

Ways to Connect

Website: thelifejournal.ca
Instagram: @_carolinecares, @caretotalkpodcast, @_thelifejournal
Podcast: Care to Talk Podcast – Available on YouTube and Spotify

Notes

The Unexpected Gift

Notes

Notes

Notes

Notes

www.ingramcontent.com/pod-product-compliance
Lightning Source LLC
Chambersburg PA
CBHW031521120626
46545CB00005B/1948